Better Homes and Gardens.®

water gardening

WILEY

John Wiley & Sons, Inc.

Better Homes and Gardens® Water Gardening

Contributing Writer and Project Editor: Megan McConnell Hughes
Contributing Designers: Lori Gould, Sundie Ruppert
Editor, Garden Books: Denny Schrock
Editorial Assistant: Heather Knowles
Contributing Copy Editor: Fern Bradley
Contributing Proofreaders: Terri Fredrickson, Susan Lang
Contributing Indexer: Ellen Sherron
Contributing Photographers: Marty Baldwin, Pete Krumhardt, Scott Little,
    Kritsada Panichgul, Dean Schoeppner, Denny Schrock
Contributing Photo Manager: Deb Wiley
Contributing Photo Researcher: Susan Ferguson

Meredith® Books

Editorial Director: Gregory H. Kayko
Editor in Chief, Garden: Doug Jimerson
Art Director: Tim Alexander
Managing Editor: Doug Kouma
Executive Director, Sales: Ken Zagor
Director, Operations: George A. Susral
Business Director: Janice Croat
Imaging Center Operator: Ben Anderson

John Wiley & Sons, Inc.

Publisher: Natalie Chapman
Associate Publisher: Jessica Goodman
Executive Editor: Anne Ficklen
Assistant Editors: Charleen Barila, Meaghan McDonnell
Production Director: Diana Cisek
Manufacturing Manager: Tom Hyland

This book is printed on acid-free paper.

Note to Reader: Due to differing conditions, tools, and individual skills,
Meredith Corporation assumes no responsibility for any damages, injuries
suffered, or losses incurred as a result of following the information
published in this book. Before beginning any project, review the
instructions carefully and, if any doubts or questions remain, consult local
experts or authorities. Because codes and regulations vary greatly, you
should always check with authorities to ensure that your project complies
with all applicable local codes and regulations. Always read and observe
all the safety precautions provided by manufacturers of any tools,
equipment, or supplies, and follow all accepted safety procedures.

Better Homes and Gardens Magazine
Editor in Chief: Gayle Goodson Butler

Meredith National Media Group
President: Tom Harty
Executive Vice President: Doug Olson

Meredith Corporation
President and Chief Executive Officer: Stephen M. Lacy

Photo Credits

Photographers credited may retain copyright © to the listed photographs.
www.aquascapes.com: 46

Limit of Liability/Disclaimer of Warranty: While the publisher and
author have used their best efforts in preparing this book, they make
no representations or warranties with respect to the accuracy or
completeness of the contents of this book and specifically disclaim any
implied warranties of merchantability or fitness for a particular purpose.
No warranty may be created or extended by sales representatives or
written sales materials. The advice and strategies contained herein may
not be suitable for your situation. You should consult with a professional
where appropriate. Neither the publisher nor author shall be liable for any
loss of profit or any other commercial damages, including but not limited
to special, incidental, consequential, or other damages.

For general information on our other products and services or for
technical support, please contact our Customer Care Department within
the United States at (800) 762-2974, or outside the United States at
(317) 572-3993 or fax (317) 572-4002.

Wiley also publishes its books in a variety of electronic formats. Some
content that appears in print may not be available in electronic books. For
more information about Wiley products, visit our web site at www.wiley.com.

Library of Congress Cataloging-in-Publication Data

LOC information available upon request
ISBN: 978-0470-91917-0
Printed in the United States of America

10 9 8 7 6 5 4 3 2 1

add the joy of water to your landscape and you will have a front seat for watching water lilies unfurl, lotuses bloom, and wildlife visiting your oasis. The following pages are stocked with inspiring images of easy-to-create water gardens and hundreds of tips and techniques to get you started.

table of contents

p.**6**

WATER WONDERS

From container gardens to streams, explore water gardens and choose the best for you.

p.**28**

PLANTS, FISH & CRITTERS

Add delight to your garden by making it an inviting spot for water lilies, koi, and wildlife.

p.**60**

WATER GARDENING PROJECTS

Use these easy-to-follow building and planting plans to create all kinds of water gardens.

water wonders

From petite tabletop ponds to babbling streams, water gardens offer rewards in all shapes and sizes. Choose a project that is a perfect fit for your home and lifestyle.

p.10
PONDS AND POOLS

Bring a pond or pool to life with the addition of fish and your favorite water garden plants. Learn about choosing the right size pond or pool for your landscape.

p.14
FOUNTAINS

The melodic sound of a trickling fountain adds a pleasing ambience to any outdoor room. Discover how simple it is to build a freestanding fountain.

p.16
WATERFALLS, STREAMS, AND DRY CREEKS

A few well-placed stones and a pump will send water coursing through your yard. Explore the variety of simple ways to move water through your landscape.

p.22
RAIN GARDENS AND BOGS

Make a positive impact on the ecology of your neighborhood with an eco-friendly rain garden or bog garden.

p.26
CONTAINER GARDENS

Don't have space for an inground pond? No problem. Create a pond in a pot, and enjoy it on your deck or patio or use it to dress up a forlorn corner of your garden.

Splash into water gardening

When surrounded by small trees and shrubs, perennials, and native stones, a new waterfall will appear to have been in place for years.

Diving into the world of water gardening can begin with barely a splash

or you can make a massive wake. The choice is yours! Even the smallest water features offer season-long beauty in the form of a glassy reflective surface or bold-hued flowering plants. Large features can be heard before they are seen when a small hidden pump creates a burbling fountain or a cascading waterfall. Simply add a small heater and you can enjoy the color and sound of a water garden 365 days a year.

Water gardens, like all gardens, are intensely personal. Customize yours to reflect your lifestyle, landscape, and love of nature.

Choose your size

From the smallest urban balcony to a sprawling country acreage, a landscape of any size can host a vibrant, lush oasis. Unlike rose gardens or perennial borders that are challenging to enjoy on a small scale such as a patio, water gardens can adapt to a multitude of spaces.

Much of a water garden's ability to adapt to a location has to do with the vessel that contains it. Sure, a meandering stream is not very practical for a rooftop garden, but a bubbling fountain would fit in perfectly. The following pages are overflowing with water garden ideas that will provide inspiration for any size landscape.

Make time work for you

There's no way around it—water gardens require an investment of your time. You cannot build or plant a water garden and then forget it for the remainder of the summer, but why would you

want to? The interactive experience of a water garden, from adding water from time to time to feeding fish or admiring vibrant-hued water lilies, is sure to invigorate an outdoor space.

Location plays a big part in minimizing the time required for maintenance. Place your water feature close to your home, along a frequently traveled path, or near a patio where you will see it regularly and can easily take a minute or two to tend it as needed. Invest a few minutes in caring for your water garden every day and it will bloom and bubble with abandon. These short sessions are guaranteed to become a refreshing—and cooling—part of your daily routine.

Consider construction

Many water features can be constructed in a few hours and involve a simple trip to the garden center and almost no specialized equipment. Others call for the expertise of a landscape architect or water garden expert, specialized earth-moving equipment, and a few weeks of intense construction.

Do-it-yourself water gardening projects abound. "Water Gardening Projects," beginning on page 60, is filled with easy-to-build projects for all skill levels. Get your feet wet—or hopefully not—with small projects such as a container water garden or a simple inground fountain, and then move on to inground ponds, streams, and rain gardens, which require more involved construction.

Above: **Call on watertight containers to bring the joy of water up close. Water horsetail, water lettuce, and water hyacinth thrive in container gardens.**

Natural benefits

As your water garden beautifies your landscape, it is making an important contribution to the ecosystem. Insects and animals are increasingly searching for water sources in urban and suburban areas, and your water garden can provide a clean, healthy source of nourishment. Whether they visit the oasis on wing or amble in on foot, you'll delight in the added dimension they bring to your space. Here are a few common water garden visitors.

BUTTERFLIES	HUMMINGBIRDS	TOADS
DRAGONFLIES	SNAILS	TURTLES
FROGS	SONGBIRDS	

Ponds

Serving as a water source for wildlife, a cool backyard oasis, the perfect spot for growing water lilies, and a landscape destination, a pond offers a multitude of benefits. Ranging from a petite watering hole to a spacious expanse of dark, glassy surface, ponds will complement nearly any type of landscape.

A cozy courtyard garden is easily home to a small inground or aboveground pond. Locate the pond near a window and add a pump and a small bubbler fountain so you can enjoy soothing sounds floating through your window. If you have a little more space, consider installing a 5- to 6-foot-wide inground pond with an informal, irregular shape to mimic a shallow water feature that you might find in nature. Add small water lilies and some floating plants to quickly bring the pond to life.

Suburban yards offer infinite pond possibilities. While ponds are often built in the backyard, a pond in the front yard is just as intriguing and likely to spur conversation between you and your neighbors. No matter where you locate your pond, be sure to check municipal regulations regarding depth and safety features. Some municipalities require fencing if the pond exceeds a certain depth.

Build a pond near your patio so you can enjoy its beauty whenever you're kicking back or dining alfresco. Or employ a pond as a destination in the landscape. Build it along or near the end of a path leading from your outdoor living area into the landscape. Add a fountain, and the sound of running water will create pleasing music and draw visitors into the garden.

Above: **Goldfish and koi thrive in ponds. Count on them to eat mosquito larvae and help prevent excessive algae.**

Opposite: **Easy-to-grow water lilies add pizzazz to any pond. Grow day and night blooming tropical cultivars and enjoy their beauty all summer.**

TEST GARDEN TIP
Add a net

Catch falling leaves in a protective net before they sink into the depths of your pond and foul the water. Spread the net over the pond in early fall and regularly remove it and toss the leaves and debris in the compost pile. Remove the net before the pond freezes.

All about ponds

One of the most popular types of water features, ponds are available in all shapes and sizes. Cost, construction particulars, and maintenance needs differ depending on the shape and size of the pond. The details below are based on a simple pond that is about 5 feet in diameter.

COST ESTIMATE
Small ponds can be installed for as little as $300 to $500 including a pond liner, small pump, fountainhead, and water garden plants. Flexible liners, those that resemble a large piece of plastic, are less expensive than rigid, preformed liners, which are often sturdier. The price of a pond increases with size, especially if extensive excavation is required.

CONSTRUCTION BASICS
In most cases, a few hours' work with a sharp spade can carve out a cavity for a lovely small pond. Excavating soil can be strenuous, especially if the soil is sticky and has a high clay content or is especially hard packed. So as not to overexert yourself, set aside a couple days to excavate a small pond—if you wrap up the task in less time, celebrate a job well done!

Sites with extremely rocky soil or hardpan, which is nearly impossible to excavate, are well suited to aboveground ponds. Created using a preformed liner, these ponds sit on top of the ground and require little or no excavation. When surrounded by perennials, shrubs, and other landscape elements, aboveground ponds are pretty and practical.

After excavating, finishing a pond is easy. You'll lay the liner, apply edging and, if necessary, plumbing, and add plants, water, and perhaps fish.

MAINTENANCE NEEDS
Ponds require attention every couple days during the growing season. Maintain water quality by skimming off leaves and plant debris from the water surface. Compensate for evaporation by topping off the feature with a couple inches of water. If you grow plants in your pond, you'll need to spend more time maintaining it, but the rewards are wonderful.

Pools

Pools, like ponds, are large reservoirs that are easy to customize for any landscape.

Unlike ponds, traditional pools typically don't have plants growing in the water. Instead the surface is clear and glassy to reflect the sky and surrounding landscape.

Pools have a formal appearance by nature, but with a little creativity you can give them a relaxed vibe. A few well-placed groupings of shrubs or perennials around the edge of a pool will soften its appearance. It is easy to add a fountain to one end of a pool to break up the fluid surface. A modern fountain will add interest to a pool while simultaneously cleaning the water so it remains sparklingly clear.

The mirrorlike surface of a pool is especially breathtaking when the pool reflects a nearby garden scene, vista, or striking bit of architecture. When deciding where to place a pool, take a long look at the trees and shrubs, buildings, and views around the space. These views will likely be reflected in the water surface.

Employ landscape lighting to highlight a pool at night. Simple electrical work combined with underwater lights or lights on the edge of the pool will make the feature a nighttime focal point. Or go green and use solar-powered lights, which are a cinch to install.

Above: **A striking aqua hue was applied to the floor of this concrete pool, giving it a vibrant, modern feel. This pool measures about 16 feet in diameter. Achieve the same look in a small landscape with a 6-foot-diameter pool.**

TEST
GARDEN
TIP

Add heat

A simple electrically powered deicer makes it possible to enjoy your garden pool year-round. The open water will become an important water source for songbirds in winter.

Left: **The arresting patterns of leafless tree branches are reflected in the glassy surface of a rectangular pool.**

Above: **A simple brick edging adds to the formality of this pool. The recycled bricks also lend it instant age.**

All about pools

Pools often have geometric shapes. Rectangles, squares, and circles are easy to carve out when excavating soil. These simple shapes maximize pond liners, avoiding the waste that is common when lining irregularly shaped ponds. The estimates below are based on a rectangular pool that is about 4 feet wide and 6 feet long.

COST ESTIMATE

Small pools can be installed for $300 to $500. Flexible pond liners are the least expensive option and the easiest to install, but they often have a shorter life span than preformed liners. Many types of geometric preformed liners that will form excellent pools are available.

Edging material is especially important when designing and building a pool. Materials costs will quickly escalate if you choose a specialized cut stone edging such as bluestone. For a lower cost alternative, consider a local stone or recycle old bricks. They can add unique color and texture to your new pool.

CONSTRUCTION BASICS

Pool construction is very similar to pond construction. Building a pool begins with excavation. Loam and sandy soil are easy to dig, and it will be quick work to carve out a pool. Clay and hardpan require a great deal of effort. Allocate one to two days to excavate a small pool.

After the pool is excavated, line it with a flexible or preformed liner. Edging material, such as stone or wood, is often used to hold the liner in place and give the pool edge a finished look. Electricity is not essential for a healthy pool, but it is easier to maintain a pool's glassy surface if an electrically powered skimmer and clarifier are integrated into the pool.

MAINTENANCE NEEDS

The most important task when caring for a pool is to maintain a healthy ecosystem so the water remains algae-free. A skimmer and clarifier will help keep algae at bay, as will simple pool maintenance such as quickly removing leaves and other debris that fall into the pool.

Fountains

Fountains are music makers in the garden.

A petite bubbling fountain creates sweet, elegant water music while a splashing multitiered fountain lights up a landscape with an energetic vibe. Fountains create a multitude of melodies. Take time to learn about as many styles of fountains as possible so you can choose the one that best complements your outdoor rooms.

A pump powers a fountain. The pump moves water from the reservoir, which may be a simple underground catch basin or a pond or other water feature, through a fountainhead. The water spills out of the fountainhead into the reservoir below. The pump then recirculates the water to the fountainhead.

A powerful pump is required if the distance between the reservoir and fountainhead is great. A powerful pump is also necessary if you want the water to make a grand splash as it cascades into the catch basin.

Fountains are simple to add to ponds and pools, but they can also be stand-alone features on a patio or balcony or in any outdoor room. Add a fountain to a container water garden or liven up a quiet corner of your patio with an urn fountain that sits on top of an underground basin.

Above: **A fountain and contemporary firepit come together in this landscape. A hole was bored through the center of the boulder to accommodate the plumbing.**

Beckon birds

The sound of moving water entices feathered friends into the garden. Create a bird-friendly garden by augmenting the fountain—an important water source for birds—with trees, shrubs, and perennials that offer food and shelter for winged visitors.

Above: **Sometimes simple is best. A very basic spray fountainhead sends water out of this fountain and back down into the reservoir in a graceful arch. The fountain complements, rather than competes with, the surrounding garden.**

Left: **Planting containers turned fountain vessels, these striking blue pots have a liquid look. This pretty fountain consists of three individual pumps and three fountainheads.**

All about fountains

Whether it is used as an accessory in a pond or a stand-alone feature, a fountain makes its presence known. Adjust the "volume" of a fountain by changing the pump size or fountainhead. The details below are based on a stand-alone urn fountain.

COST ESTIMATE

Small fountains can be installed for $100 to $200. Pumps, plumbing equipment, urns or statuary for the water to splash out of, and fountainheads are available at home improvement stores. Construction costs will increase if the fountain is located a long distance from an outdoor outlet and an electrician must be hired to run power to the fountain.

CONSTRUCTION BASICS

Fountains with inground catch basins require excavation. The excavation is much simpler than excavating a pond and requires just an hour or so of work. After the catch basin is set in place and leveled, the pump, tubing, and fountainhead are installed. Generally, a small inground fountain is a simple afternoon project.

MAINTENANCE NEEDS

Plan to top off the water in your fountain daily during the warmest days of the year. Similar to container plants, which require watering on a daily basis, fountains require water daily when evaporation is greatest. If the fountain runs out of water, the pump will be damaged, often beyond repair.

Waterfalls and cascades

Amble through a park or preserve beloved for its waterfalls and cascades and you'll be drawn to the liquid beauty of these natural treasures. It takes a small investment of time and resources to create a similar look in your landscape.

Waterfalls and cascades enliven a home landscape with motion, sound, wildlife, and a stirring sense of drama. Naturally sloping sites lend themselves to cascading or falling water. A carefully planned waterfall or cascade can turn a sharply sloping backyard into a watery respite. Be sure to carve out a terrace so you can nestle a couple cozy chairs nearby for taking in the sights and sounds of the water.

If your property is frustratingly flat, give it a lift with a berm. A mound of soil, a berm adds dimension to the landscape while creating a great screen against an unsightly view. Use a berm as the base of a living privacy fence. An irregularly shaped berm topped with small trees, shrubs, and perennials will become a lovely space for a small, inspiring waterfall. Edge the waterfall or cascade with native stones, plopping a few in the water stream, and the feature will look as if it has been there for ages.

Above: **Pleasingly tucked into the slope, this three-tiered waterfall is the perfect design solution for a sloping landscape that could be hard to manage.**

Left: **Waterfalls add valuable aeration to a pond, making it more hospitable for fish and other aquatic life.**

Above: **The turbulent water at the base of a waterfall is too much for water lilies. They grow best in tranquil water.**

All about waterfalls and cascades

Waterfalls and cascades are not restricted to grand estates. While they require a bit of planning to install and some finesse to finish with style, waterfalls and cascades are simple to integrate into any landscape. The details below are based on a waterfall that is 2 feet tall and 5 feet long.

COST ESTIMATE

Small waterfalls can be installed for $500 to $700. If extensive soil moving is required to create the "fall" in your waterfall, plan for an additional $1,000 or so of expense. Waterfalls and cascades are powered by electricity so plan to hire a skilled electrician to install the necessary power for your water feature.

CONSTRUCTION BASICS

Waterfall construction begins with excavation. The steeper the slope of the waterfall, the more rapidly the water will flow, creating a more audible waterfall. After the waterfall is excavated, install the pump, tubing, and necessary electrical work. Next lay the flexible liner. Preformed waterfall liners are available, but they often look out of place in the landscape.

Once the flexible liner is in place, situate stones along the edge of the waterfall as well as in the flow of water to slow and direct it and thus create the sound you desire. Plan to adjust the stones several times after the waterfall is filled with water to achieve the perfect water music.

MAINTENANCE NEEDS

Like fountains, waterfalls require daily maintenance. If the waterfall runs out of water, the pump will be damaged, often beyond repair. Plan to accommodate evaporation by adding water to the waterfall every day. Also, skim off leaves and other debris regularly to keep the feature running smoothly.

Streams

Well-placed stones disguise the black flexible liner used to create streams. Choose a locally sourced native stone to keep costs in check.

Streams spur water to dance through your landscape.

Whether in the form of a trickling channel or a wide canal, a stream adds movement and sound to a garden. A stream is easy to integrate into a gently sloping landscape; a significant slope may create a small waterfall within your stream, which can add to its appeal.

A stream doesn't need to be long to make an impact. An 8- to 12-foot-long stream with artfully crafted beginning and ending points will make a statement in an intimate garden. Longer streams are equally easy to build and maintain and require only additional length of flexible liner, tubing to transport water to the beginning of the feature, and a stronger pump.

Site a stream that flows where you can enjoy the sound and movement of the water. Border your patio with a trickling stream, employing wide stepping-stones or a simple bridge to cross the water. Or build a stream away from your house to draw visitors into the garden. Nestled into a gentle slope and sheltered by trees and a few shrubs, a simple water feature is transformed into a woodland stream.

Above: **Perennials, shrubs, and dwarf trees along the edge of a stream help to seamlessly integrate it into the landscape.**

All about streams

If you are able to work with the topography of the land, you can easily construct a stream in a weekend. The grade only needs to drop a few inches over the course of the stream for water to flow. The following details are based on a 10-foot-long stream that meanders down a slight slope.

COST ESTIMATE
Plan to invest $500 to $700 in a small stream. Extensive earth moving will add significantly to the cost of construction.

CONSTRUCTION BASICS
Like most water features, streams begin with excavation. Dig a shallow channel. The sides should slope inward gently to direct the flow of water. Vary the depth of the stream if you would like to create ripples and tiny cascades. After the channel is created, the next step is to install a pump and plastic tubing to carry the water back up to the beginning of the stream. Consider adding a filter to help capture debris that might topple into the feature.

Next, lay a flexible liner and use stones and logs to mask the edges of the liner, giving the stream a natural appearance. Add a few larger stones to the interior of the stream to create ripples and break the steady flow of water.

MAINTENANCE NEEDS
Streams require daily maintenance during the warmest periods of the year. Add water to the stream regularly to make up for loss by evaporation. Clean the filter regularly to maintain water quality.

Dry creeks

Embodying beauty and function, a dry creek can play an important role in managing storm water in the landscape.

After a significant downpour, a well-designed dry creek will capture rainwater runoff, slow the speed of the rushing water, and filter out soil particles before they reach the storm water system or a nearby stream.

Depending on the landscape and climate, dry creeks often live up to their name, meaning they are dry the majority of the time. Surrounding plants, the size and shape of the stones in the dry creek, and how those stones are arranged all create interest in the dry creek, transforming it from an outcropping of rocks into an artful garden feature.

Dry creeks appear the most natural when they line a channel or gully and take a meandering course. In nature, dry creeks are usually wider than they are deep. Generally a dry creek is twice as wide as it is deep. Aim to maintain this two to one ratio for a natural-looking dry creek.

Dry creeks are at home throughout the landscape. Direct water away from your foundation with a dry creek that extends from the gutter into the landscape beyond. Capture runoff from a driveway with a dry creek. Or transform a gully or wet swath of lawn into an attractive dry creek that efficiently conducts water out of the landscape.

Above: **Rocks, perennials, and small shrubs create this grass-free landscape. Small river rocks form the base of the dry creek, and large stones create an attractive stream border.**

Opposite: **Wide, shallow dry creeks like this one are best for efficiently ushering water out of the landscape. Be sure to use stones no smaller than 2-inch river rocks so the rushing water doesn't wash away the stones.**

TEST GARDEN TIP
Go local

Dry creeks require a significant amount of stone. In many areas, the most cost-effective stone is quarried locally. The color and size selection may be limited, but you can purchase the bulk of the stone needed for your dry creek from a local source and then use a few unique stones to dress up the feature.

All about dry creeks

Stone is the most significant investment when building a dry creek. Pumps, filters, and other pond paraphernalia are not required, nor is electricity. The following details are based on a dry creek that is about 12 feet long and 4 feet wide.

COST ESTIMATE
Budget $300 to $400 to build a small dry creek. The cost will fluctuate depending on the type and size of stones you use to build your feature.

CONSTRUCTION BASICS
Dry creek construction begins with excavation. Carve out the creek bed, maintaining smooth, gently sloping sides along the course of the water feature. After the creek is excavated, spread landscape fabric over the course of the creek and anchor it with stones. The landscape fabric will prevent weeds from popping up between the stones.

Set stones in place throughout the dry creek. For a natural appearance cluster small, smooth stones near the center of the water feature and situate larger stones near the edges. Partially bury small boulders at the edge of the creek, so that they appear to have been in place for years. Add plants at the edges of the dry creek, planting a few in the center, too, if you like. To plant in the dry creek, simply cut a circle from the landscape fabric twice the diameter of the plant pot. Plant in the fabric-free space.

MAINTENANCE NEEDS
Dry creeks require minimal maintenance. Plan to weed the area once or twice a month, and deadhead and prune the plants as needed.

Rain gardens

Rain gardens are beginning to catch on across the country.

Perhaps they have made inroads in your community. Functioning as a garden and a storm water management system, a rain garden captures runoff from impervious surfaces such as roofs and driveways. The rain garden holds the water, allowing it to penetrate slowly into the soil. Compared with conventional lawns, rain gardens allow 30 percent more water to soak into the ground.

Rain gardens are essentially shallow basins that fill with water only after rain. Within a day or two the water dissipates into the soil and the garden flourishes. Created using plants that thrive in wet conditions, rain gardens add structure, flowers, and fragrance to the landscape and create valuable wildlife habitat.

At the same time, rain gardens recharge local and regional aquifers by increasing the amount of water that filters into the ground. They help protect streams and lakes from pollutants carried in urban storm water—lawn fertilizers, oil, and debris and fluids that wash off roofs and driveways.

While a single rain garden has a small but important impact on rainwater management, a neighborhood effort can significantly benefit your local water system. Install a lovely rain garden in your yard and then share your knowledge and the benefits with your neighbors. Soon, your community might join you in capturing storm water and improving nearby streams and lakes.

Above: **Purple asters and native grasses thrive in this rain garden in the Midwest. Native plants are always good choices for rain gardens. They tolerate the fluctuating soil moisture with ease.**

Left: **Pretty purple Siberian iris (Iris sibirica) flourishes in moist or dry soil and blooms for weeks in early summer.**

Above: **Joe-pye weed (Eupatorium maculatum) grows about 6 feet tall, adding lofty interest to a rain garden.**

All about rain gardens

The ideal spot for a rain garden is about 10 feet from the foundation of your house, near a downspout. Water will flow through the downspout and into the rain garden. The following details are based on a rain garden that is about 5 feet wide and 10 feet long.

COST ESTIMATE

Budget $200 to $300 for a small rain garden. Plants and mulch are the only costs in building a rain garden if you do the work yourself. Reduce plant expenses by purchasing plants in small pots; plants grown in 4-inch pots at the nursery will catch up to those grown in quart-size pots a year or two after planting.

CONSTRUCTION BASICS

Building a rain garden begins with carefully siting the feature. A rain garden is effective when it is downslope from a downspout, where it can easily capture water flowing out of the spout. The rain garden should be at least 10 feet from the foundation of a home to prevent water from seeping into the foundation. After selecting the site, mark out the size of the rain garden. Make it as large as feasible.

Next begin excavating the rain garden. The typical rain garden is 4 to 8 inches deep with a level surface throughout. Mound the excavated soil around the edges of the garden, forming a berm opposite the side where water enters from the downspout. After the garden is level add plants.

MAINTENANCE NEEDS

Rain gardens require weekly maintenance during the year after planting. Provide plants with at least 1 inch of water per week so they will establish strong root systems. Watering is rarely necessary beyond the first growing season. Weed the area on a weekly basis. As the plants mature and cover the exposed soil, weeding chores will lessen but plants may need to be divided.

Bog gardens

The term "bog" often conjures up visions of a mucky quagmire

that would be an eyesore in your backyard. But pair "bog" with the word "garden" and the unsightly patch of muck becomes a thriving ecosystem that will work with the existing moist landscape conditions instead of against them.

Bogs are a type of wetland. They tend to occur in waterlogged soil that does not have standing water and therefore is not a breeding ground for mosquitoes. Many plants thrive in the soggy soil of a bog. Regionally native water-loving plants are great choices for bogs. These shrubs and perennials will thrive in wet soil and slowly multiply, blanketing your bog with plant life. In temperate areas you can grow carnivorous and semitropical plants in a bog garden with relative ease.

Bogs flourish in areas that receive at least five hours of sun a day. The land should be relatively flat and the soil can be continuously wet or dry. Like a pond, a bog is excavated and lined with a flexible pond liner. To promote some drainage the liner is punctured in a few places along the sides about a foot below the soil surface and on the bottom of the reservoir.

The edges of ponds and streams are also ideal locations for bogs. When incorporated into the edge of a pond with fish, a bog acts as a filter, enhancing water quality. Water polluted with fish waste recirculates through the bog, carrying nutrients to plants and beneficial bacteria growing there. The plants in turn clean the water and enhance the quality of life in the fishpond.

Above: **Plant a bog in a container and enjoy the unique water-loving plants up close. Moss will soon take up residence on the piece of decaying wood in the center of this pot garden.**

I have a soggy spot in deep shade at the back of my property. Is this a good place for a bog garden?

ANSWER: Unfortunately no. Bog plants thrive in areas that receive at least five hours of direct sun per day. You have a couple options. You can prune nearby trees so the area receives more sunlight or you can plant the spot with shade-loving water plants, such as many types of ferns.

Left: **Carnivorous plants, like these showy pitcher plants, add drama to a bog garden. They require consistently moist soil.**

All about bogs

Whether you use a bog as a solution to a waterlogged site in your landscape or incorporate it into a pond or stream, this hardworking water feature requires an initial input of time and effort, but requires minimal maintenance after it is established. The details below pertain to a small bog that is about 5 feet by 5 feet.

COST ESTIMATE

A small bog can be installed for $200 to $300. Bog-friendly plants account for most of the cost of a bog garden. Do not skimp by purchasing fewer plants or very small plants. You'll be disappointed with the prolonged murky appearance of your bog garden. Instead, invest in large quality plants, and your garden will fill quickly with flowers and foliage.

CONSTRUCTION BASICS

Bog construction begins with excavation. Because shallow bogs dry out quickly, damaging plant roots, bogs should be 18 to 24 inches deep. Next, line the bog with a flexible pond liner. To prevent ponding, poke small holes into the liner about 12 inches below the soil surface. Fill the liner with topsoil and plant. Be sure to soak the newly created bog well.

MAINTENANCE NEEDS

After planting, water a bog regularly to encourage root growth. Many bog plants grow and expand quickly. Be prepared to dig and divide plants every year or two to maintain a healthy ecosystem.

Container water gardens

The perfect place for beginning gardeners to dive into water gardening,

container water gardens offer nearly all the joys of ponds and streams on a small scale. Grow water lilies and tend fish in a shimmering lagoon on your patio. Delight in the soothing sound of bubbling water with a fountain on your balcony.

Container water gardens range in size from 10-inch-diameter tabletop gardens to 5-foot-diameter trough gardens and beyond. Infinitely customizable, container water gardens are easy to outfit with pumps, fountains, and plants of all sorts. And even the smallest water gardens attract wildlife. Hummingbirds and songbirds will flock to your tiny water source, especially if it contains moving water.

Any container that holds water or can be lined with a flexible pond liner to form a watertight vessel can become a water garden. Turn a pretty ceramic planting pot into a water garden by sealing the drainage hole. Flank the water garden with complementary pots of annuals and perennials and create a pocket garden.

To enjoy your tabletop and small container water gardens year-round simply tote them inside during winter months. Be sure to wait until low temperatures rarely dip below 40°F before setting the pots outside again in springtime.

Above: **Use a tabletop water garden as a centerpiece at your next alfresco affair. 'Helvola', a miniature water lily, dresses up this simple container garden.**

Tiny treasures

Dwarf water lilies are perfect for container gardens. Growing just 1 to 2 feet wide, these tiny water lilies adorn the surface of your water garden with jewel-like blooms for months in summer. Move them indoors for overwintering in fall.

Left: **Make an aquatic border for your patio with a fun trough garden like this one. A bubbling fountain adds a pleasant murmur.**

Above: **Green-leaf and burgundy-leaf water canna, papyrus, and pitcher plant are at home in a faux terra-cotta container.**

All about container water gardens

If you are new to water gardening, dip your toes in this fresh, fun style of growing plants and enjoying nature's beauty with a container water garden. You'll find that they are so inexpensive to construct and easy to maintain that you might as well begin with two or even three mini gardens. Choose containers that complement your landscape and enjoy your new outdoor decor.

COST ESTIMATE
You can build a container water garden for as little as $10. You'll need a watertight container and an aquatic plant or two. Add a small pump, specialized container, and more plants and you could easily invest $100 in a small container water garden, but it is an investment that will produce returns year-round and for many years.

CONSTRUCTION BASICS
Unlike nearly every other water garden, there is no excavation required for a container water garden. Your first task is to create a watertight container, if the container you have does not hold water. Lining the pot with a flexible pond liner is a simple way to prevent water from escaping. Next add plants and water. If the container is large enough you can also add fish and a small fountain.

MAINTENANCE NEEDS
Container water gardens require care every few days. Gardens without pumps require less care than those that need a constant water level for the pump to function. Weed and prune water plants as necessary and plan to top off the water every few days. In cold regions overwinter the container garden indoors or drain it and store it in a protected location.

plants, fish & critters

Jewel-like water lilies, striking lotuses, and graceful grasses will turn your sparkling oasis into a lush wildlife habitat. Double your delight in water gardening by making your garden a home for favorite plants and animals.

p.**30**
PLANTS

Whether they are in the water or on the pond edge, plants add color and texture to your water feature. Explore the many ways to add plants to your garden.

p.**46**
FISH

Brightly hued koi are at home in large water gardens. Goldfish and other swimmers are best for small ponds. Learn all about choosing and caring for fish.

p.**52**
CRITTERS

Water gardens beckon a variety of wildlife. Make your garden a home for your favorite birds, butterflies, and other critters with tips for creating a great habitat!

Partner with nature

Streamside plants offer nesting and foraging spaces for birds and butterflies. Wrap your water feature with perennials and small shrubs for an easy-care wildlife habitat.

In nature, ponds and streams contain checks and balances that generally maintain water quality without help.

Water gardens have those same checks and balances, but because they are artificial, they require a bit of help from you.

Good news: The glistening water lilies, darting fish, and bloom-laden pondside plants in your water garden all contribute to creating a healthy ecosystem. So these water garden gems not only add joy to the garden, but they also keep the water clean and fresh!

Sparkling water

Green algae and murky water are signs that the ecosystem is experiencing trouble. Specifically, the nitrogen cycle is not fully functioning. Nitrogen is an influential part of a healthy water garden ecosystem. The form that the nitrogen is in determines how healthy the water is for plants and fish. Too much nitrogen in the form of ammonia is deadly to fish and detrimental to plants. Nitrate, another form of nitrogen, is benign to fish and beneficial to plants.

Water gardens that maintain an active nitrogen cycle—continuously converting ammonia to nitrate—have healthy fish and plants. So what can you do to ensure the nitrogen cycle is actively converting nitrogen from a damaging form into a beneficial form in your garden? It's all about balance. Employ plants, fish, and critters to work together to create a balanced and active ecosystem.

Your best tactic is an integrated approach that looks at the water garden as a whole ecosystem. Instead of focusing solely on the nitrogen-rich waste produced by the fish in your pond, look at how other pond factors can convert the nitrogen into usable material.

The following pages highlight the plants, fish, and critters that will partner with nature to create a water garden that ebbs and flows with the seasons. A few short weeks after planting your water garden, you'll see the fruit of your labor—frogs taking up residence among the cattails, dragonflies skimming the water, and butterflies sipping from a water droplet on a lotus leaf.

ASK THE GARDEN DOCTOR

I would like to create a few small container water gardens. Do I need to be mindful of water quality with them too? Or do they take care of themselves?

ANSWER: Water quality is important no matter the size of your water garden. Apply the principles for a balanced ecosystem to your container gardens as you would to a pond garden. Too many fish in a small container quickly degrade water quality. Be sure to choose small fish for your container garden. Goldfish are a good choice.

Fish friendly **Make your water garden fish-friendly by including a diverse collection of water plants. Plants with floating foliage, such as water lilies, provide valuable shade, preventing the water temperature from fluctuating too much and stressing fish. If fish disturb your potted floating plants, discourage them by covering the potted surface with large flat stones.**

Submerged plants create underwater cover for fish, especially young fish. Many fish species lay their eggs in submerged plants. The young hatch and grow in this sheltered environment.

Types of water garden plants

Water lilies, irises, and many submerged plants help keep the water clear and the fish healthy in this medium-size backyard pond.

Great water gardens include three types of plants—

submerged plants, floating plants, and marginals. They each have a specific role in creating a healthy ecosystem. When you include at least one species of plant from each category, you're well on your way to building a water garden that will care for itself most of the time.

Even the smallest water gardens, dish gardens, and petite patio containers benefit from a planting combination that includes submerged plants (such as foxtail), floating plants (such as miniature water lilies) and marginal plants (dwarf rush is an excellent choice).

Larger water gardens offer a host of invigorating planting possibilities. If you would like to focus on flowers, include submerged, floating, and marginal plants that are beloved for their blossoms. Or go tropical by selecting plants from each category that have large leaves in bold shapes and colors. Planting your water garden is one of the greatest joys of creating it—have fun!

Frilly flowers of water snowflake (*Nymphoides* spp.) bloom a few inches above the water surface for weeks in midsummer.

Planting recipe

Use this simple guide to select plants for your water garden. When planted together in a pond or along a stream, submerged, floating, and marginal plants join forces to keep the water clean and to attract all kinds of wildlife.

SUBMERGED PLANTS
Growing underwater, submerged plants are some of the best aquatics for adding oxygen to the water. They also filter nutrients from the water, which helps control the growth of algae. Many submerged plants have colorful foliage and a few boast small flowers, which glisten under the water surface.

FLOATING PLANTS
The roots of floating plants don't require soil. They float on the water surface with their roots dangling in the water, preventing algal bloom by drawing nitrogen and phosphates out of the water. Floaters are very easy to grow and well suited to inground and container water gardens.

MARGINALS
Moist soil at the edge, or margin, of a water garden is the optimum location for marginal plants. Some grow in moist or wet soil while others grow in soil that is completely waterlogged. Adaptable marginal plants can even be grown in a perennial garden, making them ideal for linking the water garden to the landscape beyond.

Plant design ideas

Aquatic plants are a hardworking lot

with their roots filtering pond pollutants and their foliage providing sustenance and shelter for helpful pond creatures. While they are hard at work, they boast lovely blooms and striking foliage.

Designing a water garden is much like designing any other type of garden. Color, repetition, texture, and season-long interest work together to create a space that beckons you to grab a chair and stay awhile.

Play with color

Without the addition of color-rich plants, a water garden might be a dreary scene of drab brown, gray, and black. Annuals and perennials light up the glassy surface of a pond with their color-drenched blossoms, foliage, and seedheads. Whether they are planted directly in the water or dancing along the water's edge, plants partner well with water to add a colorful dimension to the space.

Color has a powerful impact on perception. Bright colors, such as yellow, orange, red, and white, are the hues that the eye sees first. Plant these attention-grabbing colors near a focal point, such as a waterfall or fountain. Cool colors—blue, green, and purple—tend to recede into the distance. When used in a small garden,

Above: **The boulders in this water garden are softened by masses of flowers and foliage from annuals and perennials.**

Opposite left: **Ring in spring with the delicate bloom of bleeding heart. Plant this hardy perennial in well-drained soil.**

Opposite right: **Easy-to-grow spiderwort blooms for weeks in summer. Plant it in soil beside your pond or stream.**

they make the space seem larger. They also have a calming quality, making them good partners for a babbling brook or a tranquil pond.

Repeat the best

Repetition in the garden creates cohesiveness. When used effectively repetition separates the water garden from other parts of the landscape. You can repeat plants, using the same species or variety or species at several points in your water garden, or you can repeat aspects of plants such as color or texture.

If repetition in the garden is new to you, get your feet wet by planting your favorite plants in clusters of three or five. This simple exercise in repetition will quickly illustrate how to generate cohesiveness and spur you to move away from planting a multitude of single plants.

Don't forget texture

Size, shape, and visual appearance as related to touch—what a plant feels like—all contribute to the texture of a plant. Create instant energy in the garden by pairing plants with different textures. Large, glossy water lily pads floating alongside spiky sweet flag is a contrasting play on texture. Lay the foundation for a calming scene by combining plants with similar textures—a collection of water-loving grasses, for example.

Texture is especially important along the shaded banks of a stream garden. Flowers are notably fewer in shade, and the green foliage that remains after the flowers fade will rise to the occasion when texture is invoked. Mix fine-texture plants, such as astilbe, with coarse-textured ones, such as hosta, for a planting that offers months of interest.

Plan a spring to fall garden

While plants in the water garden may not unfurl new foliage until the water temperature reaches 50°F or so in spring or early summer, many annuals, perennials, and shrubs planted around the water feature will come alive in early spring—even with a dusting of snow, as is the case with many hardy bulbs. When choosing plants for your water garden, put together a mix of species that adds color and texture every week of the growing season.

Remember that it is not just flowers that add interest to the garden. Colorful fall foliage, seedpods, and interesting textures can have as much impact as spectacular blossoms.

TEST GARDEN TIP

Weeks of bloom

Take the guesswork out of organizing a season-long blossom procession by tucking a few flower powerhouses into the garden. These charmers exceed the average perennial's three-week flowering window when growing conditions are favorable.

Black-eyed susan 'Goldsturm'
Blanket flower
Daylily 'Happy Returns'
Garden phlox
Geranium 'Rozanne'
Sedum 'Autumn Flame'
Spiderwort
Yellow corydalis

Hardy water lilies

Queen of the water garden, the water lily transforms a

pond or a large container garden from a simple pool with a few plants to a bejeweled oasis. Water lily's lush green, and sometimes glossy and mottled, leaves, or pads, float gracefully on the water surface and are the perfect foil for the beautiful flowers that unfurl above the water for weeks at a time during summer.

Some plants are hardy and will overwinter in the deep portion of the water garden. Tropical water lilies must be kept indoors in an aquarium or sunny window during winter.

Hardy water lilies, unlike their tropical cousins, bloom exclusively during the day. The flowers—ranging in size from 3 inches across to more than 10 inches in diameter—rise to the pond surface after the water reaches about 65°F. You're likely to see your first hardy water lily bloom in early summer. Water lilies bloom earliest in shallow ponds, which warm quickly in

spring and summer. Flower colors include shades of red, pink, yellow, and white.

All water lilies grow from a submerged crown, or growing point, that is typically 6 to 30 inches below the water surface. The crown is planted in a pot of soil that is commonly topped with pea gravel to keep the soil in place. The foliage and flowers rise from the waterlogged soil to display their splendor above the water where you can easily enjoy them.

Pair big, bold water lilies with the smaller foliage and flowers of other floating or potted plants for a pleasing combination. Water lilies offer quick pond cover and an excellent foraging area for koi and goldfish. Koi love to munch tender water lily stems. Although most water lily cultivars are best suited to small to large ponds, there are several miniature cultivars that will bloom a container garden with ease.

Above: **Water lilies commonly change color as they age. This beauty may eventually fade to a pretty shade of light pink.**

Opposite top: **Although they appear delicate, water lily blossoms will bloom for several days before declining.**

Small water lilies

Some vigorous water lilies are happiest when they have 10 to 15 feet of uninterrupted growing space. While these large water lilies don't fare well in a container garden, a host of small or miniature varieties are comfortable in close quarters. Count on these cultivars to bloom with abandon in container water gardens and pocket-size ponds.

'Froebeli' is a hardy red lily that tolerates the heat that can build up in a small water garden in summer.

'Gonnere' is a lush, double-petaled, white-flowering cultivar. Its lovely flowers stay open late into the day. It grows best in cool zones and is not recommended for Zones 8 to 10.

'Helvola' (right) is the smallest water lily available and is a true miniature with petite flowers and leaves. Its yellow blooms float on the surface and unfurl en masse among the plant's green leaves, which are mottled with striking splashes of dark purple.

'Joanne Pring' produces a profusion of little, cuplike reddish-pink flowers. It often has five or more flowers in bloom at one time.

Tropical water lilies

Tropical water lilies like it hot. Warm air

temperatures and warm water spur them to produce their multipetaled blossoms and send them to the water surface. If you think of tropical water lilies and hardy water lilies as siblings, the tropicals are the boisterous, attention-grabbing children that always want to be the center of attention. This is a great trait in the water garden!

Tropical water lilies create a pond surface that is filled with brightly hued blooms day and night. They produce many more flowers over the course of the season than hardy water lilies. An individual plant might have 10 to 15 flowers open at one time. This prolific blooming extends as long as the water is sufficiently warm. Their intense, sweet fragrance infuses the garden with perfume. Tropicals bloom in hues of blue, purple, pink, white, and yellow.

Tropical water lilies open their cup-shape flowers in the day or night, depending on the cultivar. If most of your time in the garden is in the evening after work, choose night-blooming water lilies, which open in the late afternoon and remain open well after the sun sets. If you enjoy your oasis in the early morning, go for day bloomers, which often unfurl as the sun comes up.

While tropical water lilies overwinter with ease in Zones 8 and above, you can easily grow tropicals in cooler zones. Plan to overwinter the plants indoors or treat them as annuals, replacing them every year. In warm zones, tropical water lilies bloom in spring as soon as the water warms to about 70°F. In cool zones, you might have to wait until mid- to late summer to see your first tropical water lily flower.

Above: **Purple-blue is one of the most common colors of tropical water lily blooms. Hardy water lilies don't bloom in this particular hue.**

Left: **Spur tropical water lilies to bloom in cool climates by elevating them so their crowns are only a couple inches below the water surface. They will be warmed by the sun and produce blooms.**

Above: **While the white flowers of Victoria water lily cultivars are striking, the 5- to 6-foot-wide lily pads are truly impressive. The huge leaves have upturned edges and thorns on the undersides.**

Day bloomers and night bloomers

Tropical water lilies unfurl their multipetaled flowers as soon as the sun comes up or shortly before it goes down, depending on the cultivar. Plant a combination of day-blooming and night-blooming cultivars, and enjoy the beauty of tropical water lilies whenever you are out in the garden.

DAY-BLOOMING WATER LILIES
'Afterglow'
'Albert Greenberg'
'Blue Beauty'
'Crystal'
'Golden West'
'Hilary'
'Mrs. Edward Whitaker'
'Mrs. George H. Pring'
'Pamela'
'Robert Strawn'
'Tina'

NIGHT-BLOOMING WATER LILIES
'Emily Grant Hutchings'
'Frank Trelease'
'Missouri'
'Red Cup'
'Texas Shell Pink'
'Wood's White Knight'

'AFTERGLOW'

'RED CUP'

Floating and submerged plants

Lotus

Enchanting flowers and magnificent round leaves make lotus an instant favorite of everyone who grows this water lover. Among the most ancient of plants, lotus flowers open at different times of the day or night depending on the age of the flowers. Planted in big pots situated about 6 inches below the water surface, lotuses thrive in full sun and hot weather. They need several weeks of air temperatures above 80°F to produce their exotic blooms.

Not only do floating and submerged plants help create crystal clear water,

but they also provide habitat and food for aquatic life. The underwater stems and leaves shelter fish, tadpoles, and other small swimmers. Some fish feast on underwater roots and shoots, but their feeding is rarely detrimental to these vigorous plants.

Submerged plants

Working below the water surface, submerged plants filter unwanted nutrients from the water. They improve water quality and clarity while offering texture-rich and sometimes colorful underwater foliage and flowers.

During the day, submerged plants add oxygen to the water and at night they remove it. Too many submerged plants, however, can cause the water to have wide pH swings, so in a pond with fish, keep their area to about half the size of the pond. The time to plant most submerged plants is when water temperatures reach 55 to 60°F in late spring.

Submerged plants produce few if any roots. Any roots they produce are used by the plants for stabilization rather than absorption. Grow submerged plants in 3- to 5-inch-deep containers. Cat litter trays, old seed-starting flats, and discarded baking pans work well. The container and planting media are useful for keeping the plant in a specific location.

Fill the container with sand or small gravel, and tuck a few stems and leaves into the media to secure the plant. Plant several clusters of submerged plants in one container. The plants will quickly produce roots and can be divided in a few short weeks.

Floating plants

Floating water plants are the ultimate in easy gardening—there's no potting necessary. Just set them in the water. Because they float on the water surface, these plants grow in any depth of water—from shallow container gardens to deep ponds.

Their pretty foliage and texture make them a favorite for shallow container water gardens, especially tabletop water gardens. They are also among the best filters as they compete vigorously with algae for nutrients. Floating plants shade fish from sun and provide small fish protection from predators.

Too many floating plants in a pond, however, can reduce oxygen, which harms fish. Don't let floaters completely cover the pond's surface. Remove floating plants as necessary to keep at least 40 percent of the water surface free of plants, allowing the sun to penetrate the water.

Be sure to remove nonhardy floating plants before the first fall frost or they will sink to the bottom of the pond, fouling the water as they decay during winter. Use a rake to pull them to the edge of the pond. Toss the discarded floating plants in the compost pile.

Opposite: **Floating plants offer protection for fish. The goldfish in this pond can quickly dart under the water hyacinth foliage to escape a predator.**

Above left: **The fuzzy, crinkled leaves of floating water lettuce add texture to the water garden.**

Marginal plants

Marginal plants blend streams and ponds with the surrounding landscape.

Growing where the soil is moist or in shallow water, marginal plants soften the edge of the water feature, making a smooth transition to the garden or lawn beyond. Equally important, marginal plants provide valuable food and shelter for wildlife. Birds forage among grasslike plants for nesting materials, butterflies visit flowering marginals for nectar, and insects of all types use stems and leaves of marginal plants for raising young.

Marginals can be as short as 2 inches or more than 6 feet tall. Combine low-growing marginal plants with strongly vertical types and a selection of intermediate growers for a pleasing combination of heights and textures.

Some marginals are clump forming, such as hosta, and stay where they're planted. Others are rambling types that traverse the pond edge. Many marginal plants are at home in moist areas of the perennial garden. For example, sedge, taro, and rush grow equally well in shallow water or planted in moist soil in the perennial garden.

If you would like to create a tropical vibe around your water feature or mimic the flora and fauna native to your area, marginals will help create the look you desire. For a touch of the tropics, plant water cannas with their big, bold leaves and vibrant flowers. Add taro, cyperus, and hibiscus. Native aquatic plants will blend your garden into the surrounding landscape. Natives include cattail, sedge, and several species of iris.

Because marginal plants are so diverse and boast intriguing flowers and foliage, it is easy to go overboard when selecting species for your garden. Too many varieties in a host of individual containers or along the pond edge will quickly overwhelm the water garden, causing it to look weedy. Instead, choose three to five varieties of marginal plants and plant clusters of each.

Opposite: **The thalia and rush plants in this pond grow in soil-filled pots set in the water.**

Above: **A water canna leaf is the perfect perch for a dragonfly. Water canna thrives in moist to waterlogged soil at the pond edge.**

Light up a water garden

Paint the glossy, black surface of a pond with color. Floating plants and water lilies highlight the surface of the water feature while marginal plants planted in shallow water or waterlogged soil along the edge of the pond illuminate the border. Turn on the lights with these bright-eyed plants for waterlogged soil.

CARDINAL FLOWER Brilliant red blooms in July and August lure hummingbirds. Full sun or part shade. Zones 5–11.

HIBISCUS Tropical-looking white, pink, or red flowers in mid- to late summer. Full sun. Zones 5–11.

JAPANESE IRIS Butterfly-like blue, purple, pink, or white blooms in late spring or summer. Full sun or part shade. Zones 3–9.

JOE-PYE WEED Flat clusters of mauve flowers top 4- to 6-foot-tall stems in late summer. Full sun or part shade. Zones 3–9.

QUEEN-OF-THE-MEADOW Fluffy pink blossom spikes open above lobed leaves in early summer. Full sun or part shade. Zones 3–9.

SWAMP MILKWEED Sweet-scented pink blooms top 6-foot-tall stems in late summer; attracts butterflies. Full sun. Zones 3–9.

Planting water plants

Encourage water lilies to bloom all season by adding aquatic fertilizer to the soil in early spring.

Water garden plants rely on you to make them

a nutrient-rich growing place. Unlike in nature, where they can send out roots in search of nutrients, the flexible or rigid pond liner prevents them from acquiring their own nourishment.

With the exception of floating plants, which don't require soil, and marginal plants, which often grow outside the water feature, all aquatic plants are planted in containers to keep the soil and plant together.

Pot particulars

Many types of pots are available for water garden plants. Mesh containers, also called open-weave or plastic-mesh pots, and fabric baskets are favored for filtrating plants because they allow roots to penetrate and have more contact with the water. These are the lightweight containers you often find for sale in the water garden section of a nursery.

Traditional pots such as nursery containers and clay and plastic pots with drainage holes make good homes for most water garden plants. Containers without drainage holes, especially decorative pots, are excellent for miniature ponds on a tabletop or patio.

Pot size should be matched to the size and type of plant. Because most water plants grow only in the top 10 to 12 inches of soil, that's as deep as the pot needs to be. Any deeper and the soil generally is wasted. Some plants don't need that much soil, growing only an inch or so deep. A few, such as lotuses, require a deeper pot. See the Plant Encyclopedia to learn more about the best pot for a particular species.

Soil

The best soil for water garden plants is heavy soil. Gardeners often borrow soil from their perennial beds for potting up aquatics. Traditional garden soil has many nutrients and will support good growth while keeping the plant in place.

Keep soil in place with a 1- to 2-inch-thick layer of pea gravel. The stones deter pesky fish and other creatures from digging up and munching on plant roots. If you have large koi in the pond, cover the soil surface with big flat stones to prevent them from digging in the pots.

How to plant a water lily

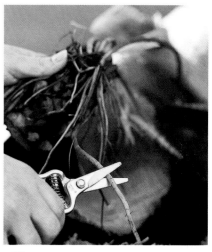

1 CHOOSE A CONTAINER
Use a container that is wide and shallow. A good size is a 12×18-inch container that is 6 to 10 inches deep. Containers may or may not have holes. If there are drainage holes, line the pot with burlap to keep the soil in the container. Soil that leaches out can cloud the water in your pond.

2 ADD HEAVY SOIL
Use a heavy soil intended for use in the garden, not a fluffy potting soil that will float out of the container. Avoid soil mixes with perlite, vermiculite, or peat for the same reason. Enrich the soil with aquatic fertilizer pellets made especially for the task. Push them into the soil before you plant.

3 REMOVE OLD LEAVES
Remove old leaves and thick, fleshy old roots. Leave only emerging leaves and buds and the newer, hairlike roots. The rhizome, which is similar to the rhizome of an iris, grows horizontally.

4 PLANT THE RHIZOME
Plant the rhizome against the side of the pot, with the growing tip pointing upward—about 45 degrees—and toward the center of the pot.

5 COVER THE SOIL
Cover the soil with a layer of rock or pea gravel to keep the soil from washing out of the pot.

6 LOWER THE POT
The planted pot should be lowered into the pond at an angle to allow air to escape. Set the base of the pot 12 to 18 inches deep. The leaves will float to the surface. If the pond is deeper than 18 inches and doesn't feature built-in planting ledges, support the pot.

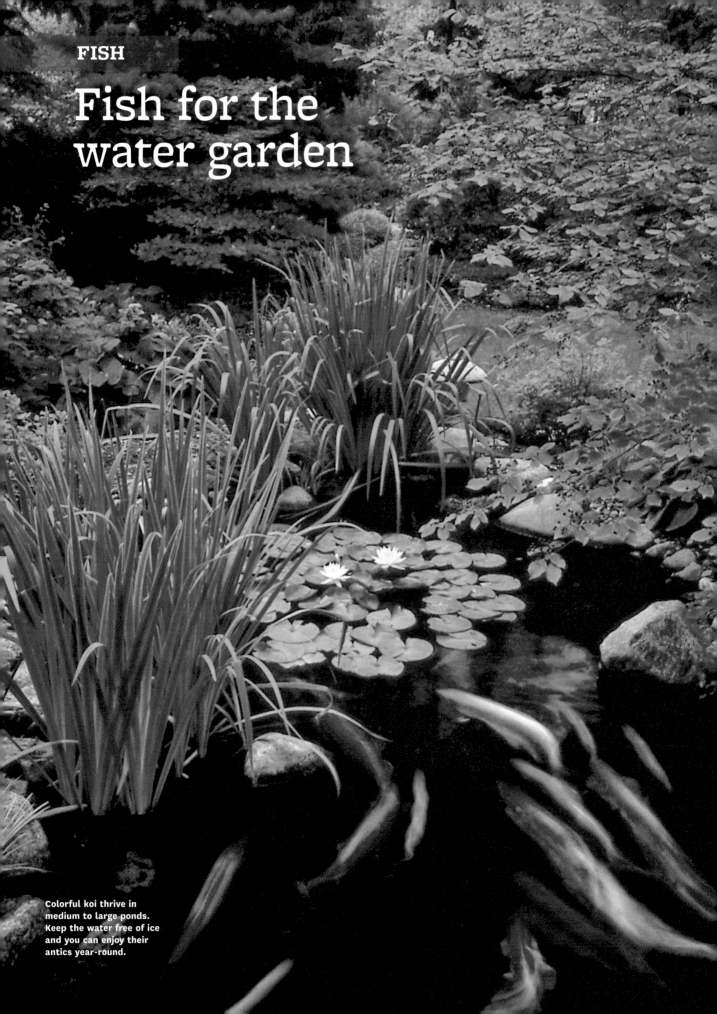

Fish for the water garden

Colorful koi thrive in medium to large ponds. Keep the water free of ice and you can enjoy their antics year-round.

Liven up your oasis with fish.
They add color and movement to the water garden. Many varieties are easy to care for, making them great pets. It is easy to become captivated by the beauty of fish and add too many to the pond at once. Instead, start with a few fish and then gradually add more of the graceful swimmers as you gain experience caring for them.

Goldfish and koi are popular choices for backyard ponds because they are large, colorful fish and are easy to spot from above. These fun and friendly fish can be trained to take food from your hand. They grow quickly, are generally pest-free, and come in many bright, cheerful colors. While koi flourish in medium to large ponds, goldfish can easily set up house in a large container garden—allowing you to enjoy their dashes and darts in a pot on your patio or deck.

Feeding your fish
Feed your fish at the same time every day, and you'll soon see them eagerly awaiting you in the pond. Give them as much as they'll eat in 10 minutes or so. Use floating pellets or flakes so that when they're done feeding, you can skim leftover food from the pond. Uneaten fish food will decompose and foul the water, leading to poor water quality as well as algae blooms.

Even if you feed koi and goldfish regularly, they may look for meals in your plants. Goldfish tend to stay small, up to 10 inches or so in length. Stocking the pond with these smaller fish will keep you from having to worry about your plants.

Koi can grow 3 feet long, and their appetite for plants is huge. To keep large koi, you'll have to take steps to prevent them from devouring the plants. When koi near 10 inches long, keep an eye on your plants. If the fish overturn potted marginals and destroy other plants, remove the fish and find another home for them.

Because koi have a voracious appetite for plants, goldfish may be a better choice for small to medium water gardens. Whether you choose goldfish or koi, be sure to add plenty of submerged plants to the pond to help maintain water quality.

TEST GARDEN TIP

Liquid reminder!
Remember, fish can't tolerate the chemicals commonly found in municipal water supplies, so you'll need to neutralize these chemicals before introducing fish to the pond. Chlorine and chloramine are the most frequently used chemicals. The good news is that removal treatments—available in the water garden section of your local garden center—work almost instantly to remove harmful substances.

Filtration fundamentals
To match the filtration needs of the pond with the capabilities of your filtrating plants and pump filter, follow these guidelines:

Goldfish: Supply at least 5 gallons of water per inch of fish.

Koi: Supply at least 10 gallons of water per inch of fish. Fish longer than 6 inches need substantially more water. Remember, koi grow fast. Do not purchase a quantity of fish based on their current size. Instead, make your purchase based on their mature size.

Types of fish

Spend a few minutes watching the antics of koi and you're sure to fall in love

with the energy and beauty fish bring to the water garden. Koi, goldfish, and golden orfe are all at home in water gardens. Just like plants, these fish help a water feature reach and keep a good environmental balance.

Koi, goldfish, and orfes

Koi are fancy relatives of the common carp. These collected and highly prized fish sometimes command sky-high prices, but you can get started with a minimum investment. Familiarize yourself with the colorful variety of koi and choose your favorite for your garden. One of the most popular categories of koi is the kohaku. These koi are white with red markings that develop as the fish ages.

Koi are quite trainable. They learn to come if you clap your hands or give some other sign on a regular basis just before feeding. Goldfish are slower to learn but they, too, can be taught to come at a signal if you have the patience to school them.

The best-known goldfish is the comet. Comets are usually bright orange-red, with long flowing fins—very similar to the goldfish you might have owned as a kid. There are two other types of comets. Those with red-and-white markings are known as sarassa comets. Shubunkins are calico-colored goldfish. The have a white body with red, blue, orange, yellow, or black markings on their scales.

Orfes are best for large ponds. They are lively, playful fish that are great for eating insects and mosquito larvae. Slender and almost bullet shape, the golden orfe will grow to a foot or more in length in a large pond. Orfes prefer to be with other fish, so do not keep them singly.

Opposite: **Koi are smart, friendly fish that will quickly learn a feeding routine and gather with gusto to get a meal.**

Joy of Koi

Flamboyant and friendly, koi bring ponds to life. Prized for their brilliant hues and distinct markings, they are seen by many gardeners as the water garden's crowning jewels. Here are some of the most popular varieties.

     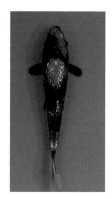

SANKE
An orange, black, and white tricolor, this koi adds flair to any garden pond.

KARASU BUTTERFLY
Japanese legend says every pond should have one black koi for luck.

YAMABUKI OGON
This shiny fish lacks the blotchy marking common to other types of koi.

KIN KIKOKURYU
Relatively rare, this variety is known for its unusual markings.

KOHAKU
Prized for its simple elegance, this bicolor koi is often the beginner's choice.

GIN RIN HI UTSURI
Metallic-looking scales give this koi iridescent sparkles in the sunlight.

Stocking the pond

When purchasing fish, the best place to shop is with someone you know and trust.

Ask local water gardening friends for recommendations. Inquire at your local garden center. Look for fish that are alert and swim freely in the tank. Avoid fish that swim sideways or those that seem to have trouble navigating. All animals should be free of spots, sores, or ulcers, and fish fins should be clean and full, not tattered or worn.

Bringing fish home

Fish are generally transported in plastic bags. For the journey home, place the bag in a polystyrene box, which will act as an insulator and reduce changes in water temperature. A sturdy cardboard box will also suffice. Keep the fish cool and in the shade. If traveling by car, don't put the bag in the trunk or in direct sunlight, where it could overheat.

Above: **Before adding new fish to your water garden, acclimate them to the water. Float the bag containing the fish in the garden. After the water in the bag is nearly the same temperature as that in the water garden, add the fish to the garden.**

It's best to take fish straight home. The longer they are in the bag, the more stress they have to endure. If the fish will be in the bag for more than a half hour or so, ask the store staff to add extra oxygen to the bag; otherwise the fish will use up the available oxygen during transport.

Introducing fish to the pond

Add fish or other creatures to the pond in early summer when the water has warmed sufficiently and before the heat of summer arrives. Don't introduce critters to the pond during excessively hot or freezing weather or during early spring when temperatures fluctuate greatly. All of these conditions stress the animals, causing them to succumb to disease or illness.

When you add a new fish to the pond, acclimate it gradually because its swim bladder, an internal organ that controls buoyancy, could expand and burst if subjected to extreme changes in water temperature. Follow these steps to add swimmers to your oasis.

Float the bag in the pond. When you float the unopened bag in the pond, the temperature of the water in the bag will slowly approach the temperature of the pond water. This will take several minutes. If the bag is in the sun, put a damp, light-color towel over it so that the rays from the sun don't heat up the water in the bag.

Add the fish to the pond. Release the fish into the pond when the temperature of the water in the bag is within 2 degrees Fahrenheit of the pond temperature. Use a net to gently remove the fish from the bag and add it to the pond. Do not add the water from the bag to the pond; it may contain diseases or chemicals.

If your fish is in a bucket rather than a bag, add some of your pond water gradually to the container so the fish becomes acclimated to the pond water temperature. Then gently net the fish and move it to the pond.

ASK THE GARDEN DOCTOR

My fish look like they are gasping for oxygen near the water surface. What's wrong?

ANSWER: Fish gasping for air, especially near a waterfall or fountain, may signal oxygen depletion, nitrite toxicity, or gill flukes (flatworm parasites). Nitrite toxicity is more common in summer when the pond water temperature soars, causing a sudden rise in nitrite levels. Lower the nitrite level and add oxygen with a partial water change and increased aeration.

Fish health 101
Keep your fish happy and healthy by practicing good hygiene in and around the pond. Healthy fish swim vigorously, have normal eating habits for the season, and greet you curiously from time to time. Promote top-notch health with these tips.

Keep the water clean. Don't allow uneaten fish food, dead leaves, or other organic debris to remain in the pond. Use a skimmer to clear debris on a daily basis. Install a net over the pond in autumn to catch falling leaves. Trim away and rake out dead aquatic plant debris.

Test the water. Keep tabs on the nitrite, ammonia, and nitrate levels in the pond with an accurate test kit. Make adjustments to the water quality as necessary to maintain healthy levels.

Treat tap water. If you refill the pond with municipal tap water, use chloramine remover and dechlorinator to remove chloramine, chlorine, and heavy metals from the water.

Attracting frogs, turtles, and other creatures

Frogs and toads are commonly seen around water features in spring during their mating season. Many will visit briefly and then take up residence elsewhere.

?

ASK THE
GARDEN
DOCTOR

**I think a
frog might
be eating my
fish. Is that
possible?**

ANSWER: Adult
bullfrogs are voracious
eaters known to devour
goldfish and koi. They
will also snatch small
birds that come to drink
or bathe. It's best to
relocate a full-grown
bullfrog to a natural
body of water.

Above left: **Turtles spend
hours basking in the sun
on flat stones. Create an
inviting space for them by
using concrete blocks to
elevate a few stones just
above the water surface.**

Above right: **Count on
snails to help control
algae growth. They also
eat water plant foliage,
but the damage they
cause is often minor.**

A healthy, balanced ecosystem is home

to a host of intriguing creatures. You'll know you have created a brilliant water feature when you spot frogs jumping into the water as you approach, and a turtle or two basking on a flat rock near the water edge. You'll see snails slowly make their way around the pond consuming debris and helping keep algae in check. And dragonflies will dazzle you by gliding over the water surface.

Employ the following tips to make your pond, stream, or container water garden creature-friendly. Or, in the case of snapping turtles, encourage less friendly creatures to seek out a different habitat.

Frogs and toads

Some frogs come to live in a water feature; others just visit to sample the local insect fare. Most toads spend only enough time in the water to lay their eggs, leaving afterward for their preferred terrestrial surroundings. They, too, enjoy munching on many insects drawn to the water and will do their part in eliminating any mosquitoes around the pond.

Attracting frogs requires little effort. Plant the edge of the pond with sedges or arrowhead to provide frogs with shade and cover. Before mowing the lawn, walk the area around the pond to shoo frogs back into the water. In cold climates, you can build a mound of twigs and leaves near the edge of the pond so the toads will have a place to burrow during the winter.

Turtles

Some species of turtles are water-loving amphibians that are delightful, but hungry, pond inhabitants. Many will munch on your goldfish and koi. They will also eat the underwater stems of water lilies and other floating plants. A medium-size pond can support one or two turtles, but a large turtle population will destroy much of the plant life in a pond.

If you want turtles in your water garden, create a separate pond just for them. You'll have to build a fence or other enclosure to prevent them from wandering away.

Snails

Snails help control algae. Some also eat water plants, especially water lilies. Japanese snails and northern ramshorn, which are about the size of a dime, and trapdoor snails leave plants alone, preferring instead surplus fish food, fish excrement, and algae growing on the sides of your pond. Snails are available from many of the same suppliers that offer fish for sale.

Dragonflies

Dragonflies and damselflies are so adept at snatching mosquitoes on the wing that they are known as mosquito hawks. They usually find ponds on their own and do not need to be introduced. Sedges, irises, and floating plants of all sorts will help draw dragonflies to your pond. They use the plants as safe places to lay eggs, and the young dragonflies rely on them for shelter.

Adults lay eggs on the undersides of water lily leaves or directly on the surface of the water. These eggs hatch in late summer, and the juveniles overwinter in the pond, even in cold climates. In spring the juveniles are carnivorous, living underwater and feeding on insects as well as very small fish. The adults live for three to four months and will guard a territory around the pond against others of the same species.

Attracting butterflies

Butterflies relish a nectar-rich garden.

Pair your water garden with a butterfly garden or a smattering of your favorite butterfly-friendly plants, and you'll enjoy a wide variety of flitting beauties. Like all creatures, butterflies need water, food, shelter, protection from predators, and a place to raise their young. A water garden and the surrounding landscape can easily satisfy their needs.

Penchant for puddles

Butterflies drink only from the shallowest puddles in an effort to keep their wings dry. The wet surface of a stone and tiny puddles created by the spray from fountains or waterfalls serve them well. Even water droplets on marginal plants are inviting.

For an irresistible butterfly attraction, create a pint-size puddle by digging out a shallow indentation in the ground near your pond. Line it with a scrap of pond liner and an inch or two of sand. Cover any exposed liner with stones. Add just enough water to keep the sand wet. Puddle visitors may include swallowtails, whites, sulphurs, blues, brushfoots, admirals, and skippers.

Some male butterflies need to drink from mud puddles in order to replenish the salts their bodies need for reproduction. Create a butterfly puddle using mud instead of sand to help the males.

Above: **Monarchs flock to butterfly weed for nectar. The plant's foliage is a source of food for caterpillars.**

You can easily set up a drinking station by filling a shallow flowerpot saucer with smooth river rocks. Place it at ground level or raised slightly on stacked bricks among some blooming plants. Fill it with fresh, cool water just to the point where water is visible between the rocks but does not cover them all. This leaves places on the rocks for sure footing while the butterflies sip.

Food source

Butterflies need two types of plants—nectar plants and host plants. Nectar plants provide sustenance for the active fliers while host plants provide a place for butterflies to lay eggs. Host plants also serve as food sources for butterfly young, called caterpillars.

Wildflowers are a favorite feast for butterflies, and a wildflower garden near your water feature will encourage them to visit often. Most wildflowers grow well in the sunny areas favored by butterflies. Choose native plants and those that are well adapted to your area's conditions. They not only will require less care from you but also will be more likely to attract local butterflies.

Shelter

Strong winds have the potential to damage delicate butterfly wings. Temper exceptionally windy sites by planting a dense evergreen or deciduous hedge. The butterflies will take shelter in the calm atmosphere and are more likely to take flight to forage.

Butterflies need a safe place to rest at night, and species that don't migrate must find a place to hibernate during winter. You can encourage them to stay near your water garden by keeping a log pile close by. A log pile closely replicates the fallen branches and trees in the woods, where butterflies naturally seek shelter. Stack layers of logs as you would firewood.

ASK THE GARDEN DOCTOR

Japanese beetles are eating holes in the plants in and around my water garden. May I control them with a pesticide? I don't want to hurt the butterflies that also call my garden home.

ANSWER: Avoid using pesticides in your butterfly garden and around your pond. Such products are not specific about which bugs they kill and will eliminate desirable insects such as butterflies in addition to the Japanese beetles. Also, pesticide runoff into your pond can kill your fish. Release beneficial nematodes and ladybugs in the garden to manage pests organically. Eliminate the Japanese beetles by plucking them by hand and plunging them in a bucket of soapy water.

Left: **Water droplets on the stones or lily pads surrounding this waterfall form perfect drinking sites for butterflies.**

Above: **Make a simple butterfly watering station by sprinkling water on a dinner plate. This shallow oasis is ideal.**

Attracting birds

Build a water garden and the birds will thank you!

A gracious change from a roadside mud puddle, a garden pond is a welcome invitation to birds large and small. From chickadees to ducks, birds rely on water for drinking, bathing, and sourcing food. A water garden abounds with insects and plants important to many birds' diets. With urban and suburban water sources becoming scarce, your water garden can play a vital role for songbirds.

Design matters

Many constructed ponds don't adequately meet birds' need for water. Often the sides drop away at sharp angles, making it impossible for small birds to reach the water. Bird-conscious construction features will make your pond attractive and safe for a wide variety of avian species.

Above: **Moving water beckons birds. Include a bubbling fountain like this one in your landscape and winged visitors will stop by to drink and bathe.**

When building your pond, create a shallow entry area, such as a pebble beach like the one shown below. The entry area can also be a shallow shelf—it should be no deeper than 3 inches—that slowly extends into deeper water. Be sure to include stones and plants around the perimeter of your water feature. These will serve as valuable perches for birds as they investigate the pond.

The sounds of running water from a waterfall or fountain will beckon all kinds of wild birds to your landscape. The source of the moving water can be very simple—a bamboo spout pouring clear water into a shallow pool, for example.

Integrate a bird bathing area into your feature. An easy way to do this is to place a large rock with a flat surface 1 to 3 inches below the water surface. Place a scrap of pond liner underneath the rock to prevent damage from sharp edges. You can also elevate a thin, flat stone by placing it on bricks or concrete blocks.

Plant particulars

Vary the height and texture of plants in your water garden to attract the widest variety of birds. Marginal and bog plants provide food and nectar for many species.

Plants around the pond are important too. Tree branches that overhang the pond by 15 feet or so allow birds to perch and check for predators before flying down for a drink. Nearby leafy tree canopies and brushy shrubs provide safe places to retreat and preen. Tall grasses and other marginal plants around the pond create places for insect-eating birds to forage. Songbirds favor plants with berries and prominent seedheads.

TEST GARDEN TIP

Year-round water

Birds need fresh water 365 days a year. If water freezes in winter where you live, consider installing an electric deicer to keep a portion of your pond free of ice. If you have a birdbath, be sure to install a deicer in it. Birds will flock to this shallow, safe spot to bathe.

Build a bird beach

Add a sand or pebble beach to your water garden to create a natural-looking and safe spot where birds can walk, bathe, and search for insects. A gentle slope into the water provides a variety of water depths for birds of different sizes.

To make a bird beach, dig out an area at the side of your pond at least 2 feet square. Leave the outer edge at the same height as the ground and make a gradual slope toward the pond that increases in depth no more than 1 inch for every 8 inches of distance. Dig the inner edge of the beach about 5 to 8 inches below the pond's water level.

Cover the excavated area with flexible liner. Along the deep edge, place a row of stones large enough to prevent pebbles from rolling into the pond beyond. Fill in the beach area with enough pebbles to create a maximum water depth of 3 inches. Add flat edging stones at the perimeter to provide a landing and preening area.

Plant a habitat

Red admiral butterflies are common backyard visitors. They sip nectar from many kinds of plants including coneflowers.

Beckon wildlife near and far to take up residence around your water feature by adding critter-friendly food and shelter to your oasis. Annuals, perennials, trees, and shrubs offer a host of essential nutrients and nesting materials for wildlife. At the same time, the plants will enhance your glistening pond with color and texture. Include a few of these easy-to-grow food and shelter plants and watch your water garden come to life.

ASTER Daisylike purple or pink flowers from late summer through fall. Valuable nectar source for butterflies. Perennial. Zones 4–10.

AZALEA Flowers in brilliant hues of pink, yellow, or white blanket these shrubs in spring. Nectar source for hummingbird and butterflies. Woody shrub. Zones 4–10.

BLACK-EYED SUSAN Drought and heat tolerant with large daisylike blooms in shades of yellow, gold, or mahogany. Nectar source for butterflies. Perennial. Zones 3–10.

BORAGE An easy-to-grow culinary herb with purple flowers. A food source and host plant for butterflies and caterpillars. Annual.

BLUEBERRY White flowers in spring are followed by tasty fruit. Put in a few plants for yourself and a few for the birds. Food source and nesting site for birds. Woody shrub. Zones 3–9.

BUTTERFLY BUSH Cone-shape flowers in hues of purple, white, yellow, or pink. Butterflies flock to this plant for nectar. Shrub or hardy perennial. Zones 4–10.

BUTTERFLY WEED Vivid summer blooms in hues of orange, yellow, or pink. Nectar source for butterflies and food source for monarch caterpillars. Perennial. Zones 4–10.

CONEFLOWER A daisylike flower with a prominent central cone. Flowers are purple, white, or shades of orange. Food source for butterflies and birds. Perennial. Zones 3–10.

CRABAPPLE Fragrant blossoms in shades of white or pink in midspring. Flowers are followed by small fruit. Food source and nesting site for songbirds. Tree. Zones 3–8.

GARDEN PHLOX Flower clusters open in midsummer in shades of pink, white, or purple. Nectar souce for butterflies and hummingbirds. Perennial. Zones 4–8.

MAIDEN GRASS Ornamental grass with many cultivars. Important source of nesting material for songbirds. Also provides valuable cover during winter. Perennial. Zones 4–10.

SNAPDRAGON Flower spikes in hues of red, white, or yellow from spring to frost. Food source for butterflies and hummingbirds. Annual.

water gardening projects

Begin your water garden today with easy-to-follow building and planting plans for gardens of all sizes. Each project is packed with ideas that can be personalized to fit your unique climate and landscape.

p.62
CONTAINER GARDENS

Create a living centerpiece with a simple tabletop garden. Or put together a larger container for your patio or porch.

p.70
FOUNTAINS

Build a fountain like this one in an afternoon and enjoy the sweet sound of bubbling water every time you visit the garden.

p.76
PONDS AND POOLS

Ponds for patios, ponds for wildlife, pools with fountains—choose one of these unique pond and pool plans for your gardening inspiration.

p.84
STREAMS

Add movement to your landscape with this stream and waterfall building tips and planting plan.

p.86
RAIN GARDENS

Protect local streams and have a pretty garden at the same time with a special rain garden plan.

TEST
GARDEN
TIP
Make it yours

For this project choose any container that does not have drainage holes in the bottom. A cast-off kitchen bowl, new garden pottery, or a found object from a thrift shop all make great vessels for this simple planter. If you plan to use it as a centerpiece as shown here, select a low container—one that is no more than 8 inches tall—so guests can easily see over it.

Floating centerpiece Dip into water gardening in a small way by setting up a tabletop garden.

Use many of the same plants you would in a larger water garden in this long-lasting centerpiece. In fact, some plants that would be overly aggressive in a large pond behave better in the restricted space of a container.

This easy-to-make garden presents a couple options for assembly. You can use all floating plants or you can use marginal plants and water lilies, which grow in wet soil. If you choose to use floating plants, the plants simply float in the water and no soil is needed. Marginals and water lilies are planted in a soil-filled container that is topped with a 1-inch layer of pea gravel. The container is then placed in the water garden.

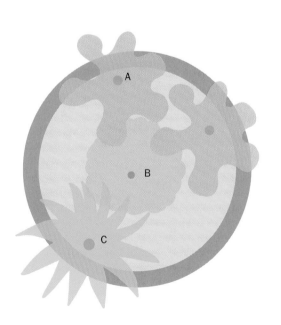

PLANT LIST

A. **2 Water lettuce** (*Pistia stratiotes*), Zones 9–11
B. **1 Fairy moss** (*Azolla caroliniana*), Zones 9–11
C. **1 Parrot's feather** (*Myriophyllum aquaticum*), Zones 6–11

TEST
GARDEN
TIP

Water smart

Irrigate container bog gardens regularly to ensure the soil does not dry out. Avoid watering so much that water ponds on the surface. Aim for soil that is moist from top to bottom. In winter you can move the bog garden inside and place it near a sunny window. Continue to water regularly. A bog garden with carnivorous plants, on the other hand, must be allowed to go dormant in winter and does not grow well inside. Overwinter it outside or in an unheated garage.

Bog in a basket If you dream of dabbling in bog gardening, this is the way to start.

An urn-shape basket holds a small, potted collection of plants that prefer to spread their roots in soggy quarters. The plants start out in the pot as small specimens and grow slowly during the summer.

The moisture-loving garden grows in a 12-inch-diameter plastic pot that has a removable plug in its drainage hole. Leaving the plug in place keeps the soil damp after regular watering and protects the basket from water damage. Bark mulch and reindeer moss provide finishing touches.

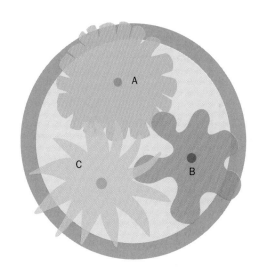

PLANT LIST

A. **Calla lily** (*Zantedeschia* spp.), Zones 8–11

B. **Red-veined sorrel** (*Rumex* spp.), Zones 6–8

C. **Dwarf horsetail** (*Equisetum scirpoides*), Zones 4–11

![Ask the Garden Doctor icon]

ASK THE GARDEN DOCTOR

Will my container water garden grow best in sun or shade?

ANSWER: Most water plants thrive when they receive at least eight hours of sun a day, but small water features like container gardens heat up quickly in full sun. The water in a 3- to 5-gallon container can easily become too warm for good plant growth. For this reason, place small container water gardens where they will receive shade in the afternoon.

30-minute container garden

A water garden is a perfect solution for a container that lacks drainage holes. Cast concrete urns both new and old often lack drainage that is essential for traditional plant growth, but they make perfect vessels for water gardening. Creating a garden is as simple as filling the container with water and adding a few plants.

Add height with lofty growers. Water lilies and floating plants hug the water surface, but a host of other water-loving plants stand tall, creating eye-level focal points. Sweet flag growing in this container is one example. Cannas grow 3 to 5 feet tall and are topped with bright red, yellow, or orange flowers.

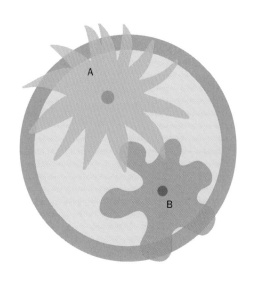

PLANT LIST

A. **1 Sweet flag** (*Acorus calamus*), Zones 4–11

B. **1 Water hyacinth** (*Eichhornia crassipes*), Zones 9–11

Front and center

A surefire way to keep any garden neat and tidy is to place it where you will see it every day. Not only are you less likely to forget about topping off the container with water and pulling weeds, but also you are sure to double your enjoyment of the garden simply because you'll regularly witness its growth. An entryway and patio are two high-traffic areas that are great for gardens.

Pretty patio collection

Invite water plants onto your patio. Lotuses are beloved for their near-perfect round leaves and sweet-scented flowers. But their rampant growing habits make them challenging to grow in small ponds—their aggressive rhizomes can quickly overtake the feature. Container gardens are a great solution.

Bring the beauty of water to your patio, deck, or other sun-filled space with this container collection. The lotus and taros growing in this collection are planted in containers that are set in watertight pots. The pots are then filled with water and become miniature water gardens.

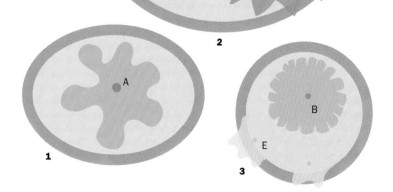

PLANT LIST

Pot 1

A. **1 Lotus** (*Nelumbo* spp.), Zones 4–11

Pot 2

B. **1 Taro** (*Colocasia esculenta*), Zones 9–11

C. **1 Water canna** (*Canna* spp.), Zones 9–11

D. **1 Creeping jenny** (*Lysimachia* spp.), Zones 3–9

Pot 3

B. **1 Taro** (*Colocasia esculenta*), Zones 9–11

E. **2 Water lettuce** (*Pistia stratiotes*), Zones 9–11

Easy-care container

Ideal for a sunny deck or patio, this container water garden is stocked with easy-to-grow aquatic plants.

When designing a container water garden, employ the same design techniques used to make a striking traditional pot garden. Aim to include a tall plant, a plant with a mounded shape, and a plant with trailing stems. In this container, water canna and cyperus stand tall, giving the container strong vertical structure. Sweet flag provides interest in the center of the container, and trailing parrot's feather spills over the edge.

PLANT LIST

A.	**1 Pickerel weed** (*Pontederia cordata*), Zones 5–11
B.	**1 Canna** (*Canna* spp.), Zones 9–11
C.	**1 Umbrella grass** (*Cyperus* spp.), Zones 9–11
D.	**1 Creeping jenny** (*Lysimachia* spp.), Zones 3–9
E.	**1 Variegated society garlic** (*Tulbaghia violacea* 'Silver Lace'), Zones 7–10
F.	**1 Parrot's feather** (*Myriophyllum aquaticum*), Zones 6–11
G.	**1 Sweet flag** (*Acorus calamus*), Zones 4–11
H.	**1 Dwarf cattail** (*Typha* spp.), Zones 3–11
I.	**1 Red-veined sorrel** (*Rumex* spp.), Zones 6–8

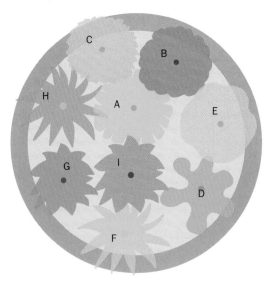

Build it **To build this container water garden you'll need a watertight container, several bricks, and aquatic plants. The galvanized tub used here is about 2 feet in diameter. While galvanized containers work well, glazed pots are fine too. Avoid unglazed terra-cotta; water will slowly seep out of the pottery.**

1 SELECT A LOCATION
Water gardens are hard to move once they are filled and planted. Take time to select a sunny location for your container garden. After you find the perfect spot, place bricks in the bottom of the container. The bricks will act as risers for the marginal plants.

ASK THE GARDEN DOCTOR

Do I need to fertilize my aquatic plants?

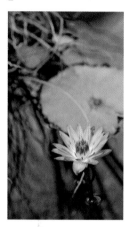

2 DESIGN THE GARDEN
Arrange the potted plants on the bricks, thinking about how you will view the containers. Situate the tallest plants, like the water canna and cyperus, toward the back of the container.

3 ADD WATER
Municipal water is just fine for a water garden that does not include fish. Fill your container garden with water, making sure to cover the tops of the plants.

ANSWER: The short answer is yes, fertilizer is generally helpful. Like all container-grown plants, aquatics that are grown in pots are limited to the soil in the pot when they are gathering nutrients. Slow-release fertilizer tablets are easiest to use, as you simply push them into the soil and they'll release nutrients over several weeks. Fertilizers with an analysis of 20-10-5 or 5-10-5 are good choices for aquatic plants.

4 TOP WITH RIVER ROCK
If potted plants tend to float to the water surface, use river rocks to weigh them down. Place a handful of river rocks around the crown of the container-grown plant.

5 ADD FLOATING PLANTS
Water lettuce will quickly establish a colony of young plants in open water surrounding the marginal plants in the tub. If the water lettuce becomes too aggressive, simply remove excess plants.

1

2

3

ASK THE GARDEN DOCTOR

Can I overwinter my container water garden indoors?

ANSWER: Yes you can. A bright sunny window is an excellent place for growing potted aquatic plants during winter. Moving large container gardens like those at left inside can be a challenge though. Consider removing the plants and water, moving each piece of the garden inside, and then replanting the container and refilling it with water.

Add height

Employ a collection of water garden containers to add height to your landscape. This color-packed trio creates an instant focal point. Creative placement of the 2- to 3-foot-tall containers will shield unwanted views or dress up the lackluster side of a house or garage. Amplify the height of the containers by filling them with tall aquatic plants such as arrowhead and water canna.

Tall containers like these do present a challenge—most aquatic plants grow best when they are a few inches below the water surface. Support potted aquatic plants by filling the container with bricks, cement blocks, or river rocks. Set the potted plants on the filler material.

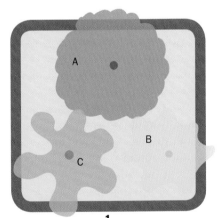

1

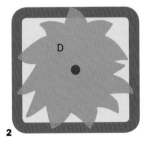

2

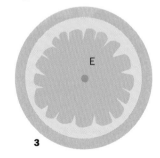

3

PLANT LIST

Pot 1

A. **1 Arrowhead** (*Sagittaria latifolia*), Zones 5–11

B. **1 Water hyacinth** (*Eichhornia crassipes*), Zones 9–11

C. **1 Lesser spearwort** (*Ranunculus flammula*), Zones 5–9

Pot 2

D. **1 Copperleaf** (*Alternanthera reineckii*), annual

Pot 3

E. **1 Water plantain** (*Alisma plantago*), Zones 5–8

TEST GARDEN TIP

Sparkle power

Glass balls are a fun way to add bling to water gardens. Add them to ponds or containers, like the ones at left, and your garden will glisten with additional color as the balls reflect the sun. Find glass balls at your local garden center or home improvement store.

Quick care garden

Water gardening in a container is the way to go if you are away from home for extended periods. This easy-care collection only requires topping off with water every few days when the water level dips. If you will be away for several days, move the pots to a shaded location, add plenty of water, and they'll grow with gusto.

PLANT LIST

Pot 1

A. **1 Umbrella grass** (*Cyperus papyrus*), Zones 9–11

B. **1 Water hyacinth** (*Eichhornia crassipes*), Zones 9–11

C. **1 Copperleaf** (*Alternanthera reineckii*), annual

Pot 2

D. **1 Water lettuce** (*Pistia stratiotes*), Zones 9–11

E. **1 Elephant's ear** (*Alocasia* spp.), Zones 10–11

Pot 3

F. **1 Arrowhead** (*Saggitaria latifolia*), Zones 5–11

G. **1 Houttuynia** (*Houttuynia cordata*), Zones 5–11

H. **1 Lesser spearwort** (*Ranunculus flammula*), Zones 5–9

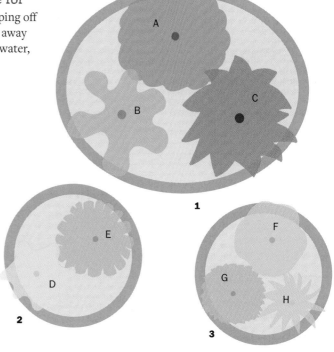

Ring around a fountain

Light up a shade garden with an easy-care fountain and annuals.

Impatiens and polka-dot plant dazzle with splashes of cream and pink while the terra-cotta pot fountain provides a focal point. Caring for this pocket garden is as easy as watering the plants every other day or so and topping off the fountain when the water level drops.

Make a fountain by coating a large clay pot with deck sealant and adding a small pump. Feed the pump's cord through the drainage hole and seal the hole with caulk. Conceal the cord under mulch. Allow the caulk to cure for two days, fill the pot with water, turn on the pump, and enjoy!

PLANT LIST

A. **32 Impatiens** (*Impatiens walleriana*), Annual

B. **9 Polka-dot plant** (*Hypoestes phyllostachya*), Annual

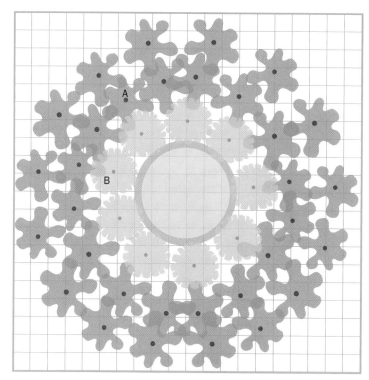

A

B

1 square = 3 inches

Watch the water level

Low water spells trouble for pumps. If a pump functions out of water, it will quickly seize, often fatally damaging the internal workings. Safeguard against such a loss by investing in a pump that has a low water shut-off. When it senses a low water level, it will automatically shut off before damage occurs.

Building tips

Make your own splash. Change the fountainhead and give the fountain a different look. A simple bubbler fountainhead is used here. You could also use a bell-shape head or a short geyser head. Prevent excessive water loss due to wind and evaporation by choosing a spray pattern and pump that elevate water no more than 10 to 12 inches above the water surface.

Great color for shade. It can be difficult to find colorful annuals for shady areas. The impatiens and polka-dot plants featured in this plan are excellent choices. Here are a few more. Wishbone flower (*Torenia fournieri*) grows about a foot tall and has bicolor flowers in shades of blue, purple, pink, or white with a splash of yellow in the throat. Wax begonia (*Begonia × semperflorens-cultorum*) has shiny green foliage and clusters of pink, red, or white flowers. Coleus (*Solenostemon scutellarioides*), shown at right, has lovely foliage marked in various combinations of green, white, red, burgundy, and yellow.

Choose another center of interest. This garden is adaptable to your landscape. If the terra-cotta fountain doesn't meld well with your space, add a different centerpiece. Purchase a ready-made fountain or birdbath for the center of the garden. Elevate it, if necessary, by setting it atop a stack of bricks or pavers.

Go perennial. Annuals add bold, season-long color, but they must be replanted every spring. Perennials offer color and texture without the regular springtime planting. Great perennials for shade include astilbe, black snakeroot (*Cimicifuga racemosa*), bleeding heart (*Dicentra spectabilis*), and brunnera.

TEST
GARDEN
TIP

Quick care tips

A great low-maintenance garden feature, a bubbling fountain is easy to care for in summer. Simply add water every day or two. In winter, move the fountain inside to protect it from the elements. Disassemble it and store it in a shed or garage. Or leave it assembled and enjoy it indoors.

Bubbling sphere
The natural good looks of terra-cotta combined with the soft sounds of water make this easy-to-build feature perfect for any area of the garden. Set the self-contained fountain in a garden bed, on top of a pretty stone pedestal, or on a table. As it stands outside, the sphere will acquire a weathered mossy coat. Be sure to choose a high-fired terra-cotta sphere that can withstand prolonged exposure to water.

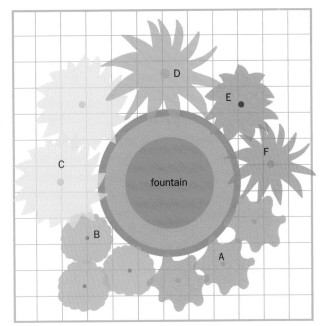

1 square = 3 inches

PLANT LIST	
A.	**3 Impatiens** (*Impatiens walleriana*), annual
B.	**3 European wild ginger** (*Asarum europaeum*), Zones 4–9
C.	**2 Liriope** (*Liriope muscari*), Zones 5–11
D.	**1 Kangaroo paw** (*Anigozanthos* Bush Gem Series), Zones 9–10
E.	**1 Coleus** (*Solenostemon scutellarioides*), annual
F.	**1 Hummingbird mint** (*Agastache cana*), Zones 5–9

Build it To build this bubbling sphere you'll need the following materials: a large terra-cotta bowl with a drainage hole in the bottom, pond liner, a wide terra-cotta saucer that will fit in the bottom of the terra-cotta bowl, a small submersible pump, a terra-cotta sphere, flexible plastic tubing, and a bag of pea gravel.

1 LINE THE BOWL
Line the bowl with flexible pond liner. Allow for several inches of excess around the top of the bowl. You will trim the excess when you finish the project. Set the pump in the bottom of the lined bowl.

2 ADD THE SAUCER
Using a carbide-tip or masonry bit attached to a drill, make several holes in the bottom of the saucer for drainage. Drill one hole in the center large enough to house the plastic tubing and a hole along the edge for the pump's electrical cord. Place the saucer upside down in the bowl.

3 DRILL THE SPHERE
Using a drill bit slightly larger than the diameter of the plastic tubing, make a hole in the top center of the sphere. Make another hole in the bottom center of the sphere.

4 THREAD THE TUBING
Feed the tubing through the center hole in the saucer, attaching it to the pump. Feed the other end through the hole in the bottom of the sphere.

5 PLACE THE SPHERE
Center the sphere on the upside-down saucer. Gently tug on the tubing so it runs straight up from the pump through the saucer and out the sphere's top. Check the pump by filling the bowl with water and plugging in the unit. If everything works, trim the end of plastic tubing just above with the sphere.

6 FINISH WITH GRAVEL
Wash the pea gravel to remove silt and grit. Fill the bowl with gravel. Adjust the liner so it is laid evenly, with no low spots along the edge. Trim excess liner to the edge of the bowl. The gravel should conceal the liner.

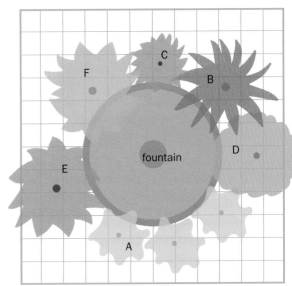

My fountain is losing water. What's wrong?

ANSWER: If water loss becomes a problem with your fountain, there are two likely causes. First, if the reservoir is not perfectly level, water will slowly seep out over time and the fountain will not function properly. The second cause of low water might be wind. The spray of excessively tall or active fountains is easily displaced by strong wind, resulting in water loss from the reservoir. Mitigate water loss by planting evergreen shrubs nearby to block the wind. Also, consider switching to a low-profile fountainhead, such as the bell-shape head in this project.

Simple bell fountain

Add the sound of water to your patio with this easy-to-install inground pool and fountain. An underground reservoir captures the water and houses the pump and components that make this pretty fountain function. A safe water feature for homes with small children, the fountain and its covered reservoir reduce safety concerns while still offering the joy of moving water in the landscape.

Personalize your fountain by using any fountainhead you like. A bell-shape fountainhead is used here, but the step-by-step process is the same for any fountainhead you choose. Create more splash and drama with a geyser or multitiered sprayhead. If you would like to turn an urn or other decorative object into a fountain, simply run the vinyl tubing through the vessel rather than attaching a fountainhead.

PLANT LIST

A.	**3 Bugleweed** (*Ajuga reptans*), Zones 3–11
B.	**1 Astilbe** (*Astilbe* 'Deutschland'), Zones 4–8
C.	**1 Purple fountain grass** (*Pennisetum setaceum* 'Rubrum'), annual
D.	**1 Ligularia** (*Ligularia dentata*), Zones 4–8
E.	**1 Astilbe** (*Astilbe* 'Red Sentinel'), Zones 4–9
F.	**1 Variegated hosta,** such as 'Fire and Ice,' Zones 3–9

1 square = 3 inches

Build it

You can build this fountain in an afternoon. Begin by gathering the following supplies: preformed pond liner, sand, rigid PVC pipe long enough to extend from the fountain to the nearest electrical outlet, fountainhead, pump, window screening, heavy-duty resin grate, concrete block, zip ties, hose clamp, and river rock.

1 EXCAVATE
Dig a hole slightly larger than the preformed pond liner and 1 inch deeper. A preformed liner should fit snugly in the excavated space. As you dig, check every so often to ensure fit. For easy cleanup have a tarp or wheelbarrow nearby in which to toss the excavated soil. Spread 1 to 2 inches of sand in the bottom of the hole.

2 CHECK THE LEVEL
Check that the liner sits level in the hole. A water feature that is not level will slowly leak water and require constant topping off.

3 BACKFILL
Backfill around the liner with fine soil, checking the level of the liner as you work. Occasionally tamp the backfill with the shovel handle to firm the soil and eliminate air pockets.

4 ADD ELECTRIC
Dig a 2-inch-deep trench from the electrical outlet to the liner. Thread the pump cord through PVC pipe, place the pipe in the trench, and cover with soil. Be sure the outlet you are using has a ground fault circuit interrupter (GFCI) to protect against electrical shock.

5 ATTACH THE PUMP
Simply attach the fountainhead to the pump, or if using an urn, attach vinyl tubing to the pump with a hose clamp (shown above). Protect the pump from debris by wrapping it loosely with window screening.

6 PREPARE THE BASIN
Place a concrete block and rocks in the bottom of the liner. Prepare the grate by cutting a door in its center with a jigsaw. The door should be only large enough to place the pump in the liner and allow the fountain to rise above the grate. When setting up an urn fountain, leave off the door and attach it to the grate with zip ties. Place the grate over the liner.

7 ADD THE PUMP
Lower the pump into the reservoir and onto the concrete block. Add flat rocks to achieve the desired fountain height. Fill the liner with water, then test the pump, adjusting water flow to prevent excessive splashing. For an urn fountain, close the door with the tubing snaking out through the grate and into the urn. Finish by topping the grate with a layer of river rock.

ASK THE GARDEN DOCTOR

I have a bog near my pond. I was on vacation for about a week and when I came back my bog plants were shriveled and limp. What happened?

ANSWER: It sounds as if your bog dried out while you were away. Dry soil spells quick death for moisture-loving plants. Prevent your bog from drying out by watering it just as you water your container plantings. Aim to water bog plantings every other day or so during summer.

Petite pond

Build this tiny pond and you'll give a valuable gift to a host of creatures in your neighborhood. Even the smallest ponds teem with frogs, snails, and insects of all kinds. Birds and other small garden visitors will stop by for refreshment, thanks to the lush plantings and moist environment. Situate your pond garden next to a patio or deck where you can easily watch local wildlife.

Many water-loving perennials thrive in shallow ponds. For a pond with a pronounced tropical flair, include water cannas, hibiscus, and papyrus. A pond garden in the Midwest or Northeast will take on a natural appearance when you incorporate cattails, cardinal flower, and Louisiana iris.

In this garden, the giant arrow-shape leaves of taro provide the focal point. A tender tropical, taro is hardy in Zones 9 to 11. You can overwinter it by transferring it to a tub of water in a location where the temperature stays above 50°F. This overwintering technique can be used with many other tropical water garden plants including lotuses and tropical water lilies.

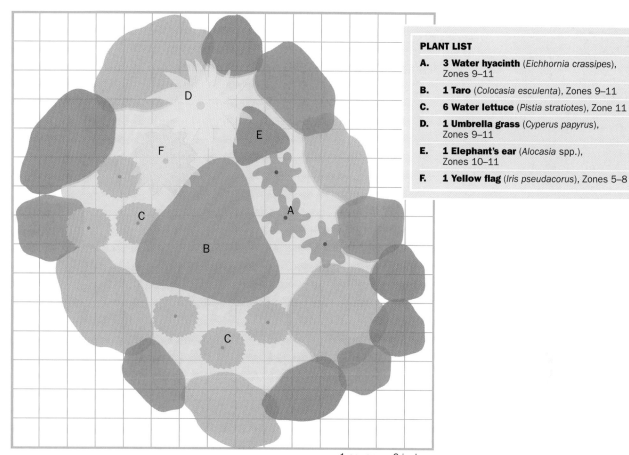

PLANT LIST

A. **3 Water hyacinth** (*Eichhornia crassipes*), Zones 9–11

B. **1 Taro** (*Colocasia esculenta*), Zones 9–11

C. **6 Water lettuce** (*Pistia stratiotes*), Zone 11

D. **1 Umbrella grass** (*Cyperus papyrus*), Zones 9–11

E. **1 Elephant's ear** (*Alocasia* spp.), Zones 10–11

F. **1 Yellow flag** (*Iris pseudacorus*), Zones 5–8

1 square = 6 inches

Building tips

Consider a preformed pond liner. Preformed pond liners are ideal for small ponds. Available in many different shapes, these all-in-one units are easy to install and rarely leak. Lasting 20 years or longer, a preformed liner is a long-term investment.

Include a variety of plants. Even small ponds can support a diverse collection of plants. Aim to include submerged, floating, and marginal plants in your petite pond. Because the garden is small, you need to be vigilant about removing excessive foliage to maintain open water, but the extra effort will pay off with a healthy pond ecosystem.

Add drama with a fountain. A small bubbler fountainhead will add intriguing motion and sound to your little oasis. The sound is likely to attract critters, making your habitat rife with colorful birds and butterflies. The fountain will also incorporate additional oxygen into the water, promoting excellent water quality.

Wrap your pond with perennials. Don't stop planting at the pond edge. Plant a swath of nectar-rich perennials around the edge of your water feature to further encourage butterflies and beneficial insects to take up residence. Easy-care perennials include bee balm (*Monarda didyma*), shown at right, butterfly weed (*Asclepias tuberosa*), and catmint (*Nepeta racemosa*).

Pond in a weekend

Small enough to cozy up to a patio in a modest backyard, this simple pond is a haven for wildlife, plants, and people. A gentle stream of water falls into the pond every few minutes from the bamboo fountain. A great pond for your first inground water garden project, it is large enough to support fish. Goldfish, such as shubunkins and comets, are good candidates. In cold climates add a simple deicer to the pond in winter and safely overwinter fish in the pond.

PLANT LIST

A.	**1 Japanese maple** (*Acer palmatum*), Zones 6–8
B.	**4 Hosta** (such as *Hosta* 'Patriot'), Zones 3–9
C.	**3 Daylily** (*Hemerocallis* spp.), Zones 3–11
D.	**4 Maiden grass** (*Miscanthus sinensis* 'Gracillimus'), Zones 4–10
E.	**6 Japanese spiraea** (*Spiraea japonica* 'Magic Carpet'), Zones 4–9
F.	**1 Dwarf hardy water lily** (*Nymphaea* spp.), Zones 4–9
G.	**1 Dwarf cattail** (*Typha* spp.), Zones 3–11

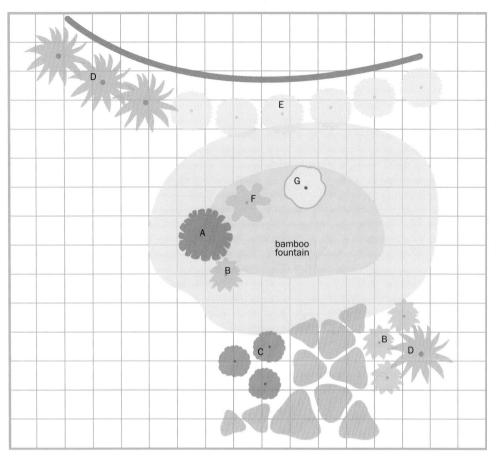

bamboo fountain

1 square = 1 foot

TEST
GARDEN
TIP

Fish facts

If you choose to stock fish in your pond, remember to stop feeding them when the water temperature is below 50°F. Overfeeding fish in spring and fall leads to a deadly buildup of ammonia when nitrifying bacteria slack off in cool temperatures. Reducing fish food waste in the pond along with skimming off fallen leaves and other debris will help the pond reach a healthy balance of beneficial bacteria.

Building tips

Include a shelf. Begin by outlining the shape of the pond and the circular path around the outside. When excavating the pond, dig a shelf about 4 inches deep and 6 inches wide around the perimeter. If you dig your pond more than 2 feet deep, you may need to fence your yard; check local zoning regulations.

Soften the liner. After the underlayment (see page 129) is in place, lay the flexible liner. Liner is easier to work with if you allow it to warm and soften in the sun for about an hour before you lay it in the pond. Pleat and tuck the liner around the edges of the pond. Hold it in place with large stones.

Disguise the liner. Place rocks along the edge of the pond to permanently hold the liner in place and to camouflage it once the pond is filled. Here, medium round river stones were used. After placing the large stones, cut off excess liner with a heavy-duty utility knife, leaving about 1 foot of liner extending beyond the rocks.

Fill the gaps. After the pond is edged with medium and large stones, the liner will still be visible. Sprinkle pea gravel between the stones to fill any gaps. Fill the pond, adding water until it is 1 inch above the bottom of the large rocks ringing the pond.

Add power. Finish the pond by installing the pump and bamboo fountain. Run the electrical cord out of the pond between the rocks. If necessary, connect it to a heavy-duty extension cord. For safety, thread the extension cord through a PVC pipe. Bury the pipe in a 6-inch-deep trench. Connect the cord to an outlet with a ground fault circuit interrupter (GFCI).

TEST GARDEN TIP

Choose your stone

Mortared granite cobblestones add to the old-world charm and stately appearance of this formal pool. You can achieve a similar look with brick or cut flagstone. To unify a pool with other areas of your landscape, employ a material that is used on a patio or walkway.

Formal affair

Playing off the geometry of nearby brick walls and paths, this pool and fountain reflect the classic styling of their surroundings. The large lava rock fountain in the center of the pool is the perfect cooling element for steamy summer days and will add sound and movement to the landscape all year long.

A pump and simple plumbing techniques can transform a variety of items—from a ceramic urn to a special piece of art to a funky found object—into a fountain. Select an object that is meaningful to you and turn it into a trickling backyard fountain.

PLANT LIST	
A.	**2 Thalia** (*Thalia dealbata*), Zones 7–11
B.	**1 Hardy water lily** (*Nymphaea* spp.), Zones 4–10
C.	**5 Azaleas** (*Rhododendron* spp.), Zones 4–9
D.	**3 Deciduous trees, such as Callery pear** (*Pyrus calleryana*), Zones 5–8
E.	**24 Liriope** (*Liriope* spp.), Zones 5–11

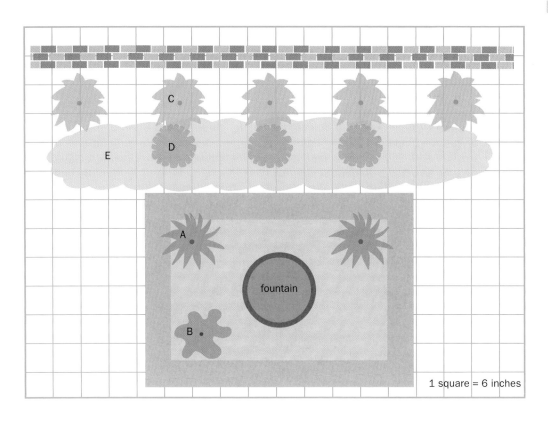

ASK THE
GARDEN
DOCTOR

Is there a way to discourage mosquitoes in and around my pool?

ANSWER: Goldfish, frogs, and dragonflies eat mosquito eggs, which reduces the population of biting adults. You may want to try a commercial product called Mosquito Dunks. The round pellets dissolve in the water and release a biological pesticide that prevents mosquito larvae from developing.

1 square = 6 inches

Building tips

Get the most out of your pool. Careful site selection will ensure that your pool is more than a lovely landscape feature. Situate it near a favorite outdoor living area, such as your patio or deck, so you can enjoy it every time you are outside. Include a fountain near your home so you can enjoy the sound of moving water anytime the windows are open.

Invest in a pump with an integrated UV clarifier. It can pump water and clarify it at the same time. Available at home improvement stores, a multitasking pump is a smart investment that will reduce maintenance.

Think ahead about electricity. Fountains are powered by pumps, and pumps draw electricity from GFCI outlets. A mortared edge like the one on this pool demands that you think ahead about how the cord will extend out of the pool to the outlet. Eliminate tripping hazards and make pump replacement easy by threading the cord through a length of PVC pipe and then burying the pipe and building the pool edge over it.

Hire a mason. Get the polished look of a mortared edge by employing the skills of a mason. With a few specialized tools or skills, you can easily build a pool, but a mortared edge like the one on this feature requires some professional know-how and experience.

ASK THE GARDEN DOCTOR

I think my koi are knocking over the potted water lilies in my pond. What can I do?

ANSWER: It sounds like koi are after the succulent water lily stems. Protect the stems and add valuable weight to the pots by placing bricks on the soil surface around the water lily stems. The koi might still be able to munch some parts of the plants but they most likely won't be able to topple the heavy containers.

Welcome wildlife

Designed with wildlife in mind, this beautiful oasis is home to fish, frogs, and a bevy of other aquatic animals and insects. Pond plants provide sheltering shade for the fish and encourage frogs and dragonflies to take a rest on their leaves. The small waterfall at the far end of the pond oxygenates the water to create a healthy ecosystem, and its rippling sound attracts birds.

For optimal wildlife health, be vigilant about water quality. Remove spent flowers, yellowing foliage, and excess plant growth. Rake off overexuberant floating plants, especially if they cover more than 60 percent of the water's surface, so sunlight can penetrate the water. Be sure not to overfeed fish. Excessive fish food in pond water leads to algae bloom.

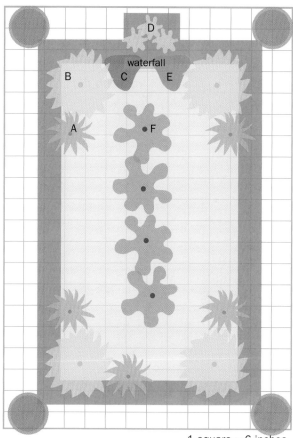

1 square = 6 inches

PLANT LIST

A. **5 Umbrella grass planted in individual large black plastic pots** (*Cyperus alternifolius*), Zones 9–11

B. **12 Sweet flag planted in 4 large black plastic tubs** (*Acorus calamus*), Zones 4–11

C. **1 Purple-leaf taro** (*Colocasia esculenta*), Zones 10–11

D. **3 Water hyacinth** (*Eichhornia crassipes*), Zones 9–11

E. **1 Green-leaf taro** (*Colocasia esculenta*), Zones 10–11

F. **4 Tropical water lily** (*Nymphaea* spp.), Zones 9–11

Building tips

Dig deep. Overwinter fish in a pond by building deep enough that the pond does not freeze. In warm southern climates, a pond that is 2 feet deep is sufficient; northern climates require a depth of 3 to 4 feet greater to ensure the water does not freeze completely.

Add a shelf. A plant shelf around all or part of the pond offers many benefits. Located 8 to 12 inches below the water's surface, the planting shelf is the perfect place for growing yellow flag, cyperus, and other marginal plants that don't thrive in deep water.

Keep the waterfall small. A small-scale waterfall, with a rise of 6 to 8 inches, like the one in this design, offers great benefits to wildlife but does not splash so much that the foliage of water lilies and other pond plants gets wet.

Invest in a filter and UV clarifier. Ease maintenance chores, especially if you plan to have fish in the pond, by installing a filter and UV clarifier. Be sure both units are rated to function in your pond's water volume.

TEST GARDEN TIP

Small space solution

A great attribute of water gardens is that they blend well into almost any landscape. If you have a tiny backyard and little or no space for a patch of grass between your deck or patio and the stream beyond, simply build the stream alongside the patio. The stream will finish the patio in style and bring the sound of running water closer to your home. If you live in a busy neighborhood with lots of traffic, the pleasing sound of water will mask the buzz of cars zipping by, creating a more relaxing outdoor room.

Flowing border
Wrapping the backyard in shimmering beauty, a babbling brook and adjoining pond bring the joys of nature close to the patio. Separated from the patio by a swath of grass, the water feature draws guests into the landscape, encouraging them to take a closer look at the fish gliding through the water in the pond. Small shrubs and trees grow behind the meandering stream and pond to further enclose the outdoor living area.

A neatly maintained edging between the lawn and water garden will enhance the overall look of your landscape. Prevent turf from sending roots into soil along the pond edge by installing a metal or plastic barrier—called landscape edging—about 1 foot beyond the edge of the water feature. The landscape edging will confine the turf, keeping mowing chores simple and eliminating the tedious task of clipping grass that grows between stones edging the water feature.

PLANT LIST

A. **1 Umbrella grass** (*Cyperus* spp.), Zones 9–11

B. **1 Rush** (*Juncus* spp.), Zones 4–9

C. **6 Shade-loving annuals, such as begonia and impatiens**

D. **5 Ferns** (*Osmunda* spp.), Zones 3–8

E. **10 Shade-loving perennials, such as heart-left brunnera** (*Brunnera macrophylla*), Zones 3–10, and **astilbe** (*Astilbe* spp.), Zones 4–8

F. **4 Deciduous trees, such as flowering dogwood** (*Cornus florida*), Zones 5–8, and **crabapple** (*Malus* spp.), Zones 5–8

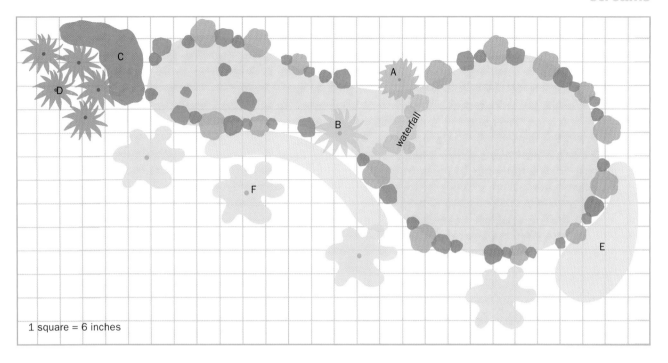

C
D
A
waterfall
B
F
E

1 square = 6 inches

Building tips

Keep good soil. Every stream and pond excavation yields some valuable topsoil. Save this black gold for use in other areas of your landscape. Fill low spots with a 3- to 4-inch layer of soil or use the excess to promote good drainage around your foundation. You can also form the soil into a berm and make a living screen of drought-tolerant plants.

Be mindful of waterfall height. The height of a waterfall dictates the amount of sound it produces. Tall waterfalls are louder than short falls. If your stream and waterfall are positioned close to an outdoor room where you gather with friends for alfresco meals and kicking back, opt for a waterfall that is only 1 foot tall or less so you can easily converse over the sound of the water.

Take your time with stone. Positioning stone around a water feature is an art. As you build your feature, take your time. After positioning the first round of large boulders and stones, step away from the project and live with the results for a day or two. Consider how you might like to reposition the stones. Once you are happy with the results, add the small and medium stones. Giving yourself time to analyze the project as it comes together ensures better results.

Easy rain garden

A rain garden is a great friend of Mother Nature. These shallow depressions capture runoff, allowing water to slowly drain into the soil instead of quickly flowing into the storm water system or other path of least resistance. Any sediment that flows into the natural water ways is captured in the rain garden, helping to keep ponds and streams clean.

Rain gardens can capture runoff from roofs, driveways, hillsides, and even streets. This adaptable rain garden plan was installed about 10 feet away from the foundation of a house, but it could easily be placed near the end of a driveway or in a shallow depression near the bottom of a hill. A simple dry creek ushers water from the nearby gutter outlet to the rain garden. A rock-lined dry creek like this one is not necessary for creating a rain garden, but it anchors the rain garden in the landscape, making it a destination.

Go native when choosing plants for your rain garden. This planting plan is filled with Midwest prairie species and a few exceptional water-tolerant and drought-tolerant species that thrive in many regions. Native plants develop deep root systems, allowing them to source water when the rain garden is dry for extended periods. The deep root systems also help build and maintain high organic matter content in the soil and porosity so water can infiltrate. Contact your local extension service to learn about native species for your region.

PLANT LIST

A. **2 Cardinal flower** (*Lobelia cardinalis*), such as 'Compliment Deep Red', Zones 3–9

B. **1 False indigo** (*Baptisia australis*), such as 'Midnight', Zones 3–10

C. **6 Purple prairie clovers** (*Dalea purpurea*), Zones 3–9

D. **3 Prairie dropseed** (*Sporobolus heterolepis*), Zones 3–9

E. **3 Calamint** (*Calamintha nepeta* ssp. *nepeta*), Zones 5–9

F. **1 Golden groundsel** (*Ligularia dentata*), such as 'Britt-Marie Crawford', Zones 4–8

G. **1 Pink turtlehead** (*Chelone lyonii* 'Hot Lips'), Zones 4–10

H. **1 White snakeroot** (*Eupatorium rugosum*), such as 'Chocolate', Zones 4–9

I. **3 Gayfeather** (*Liatris spicata*), such as 'Floristan Violet', Zones 3–10

J. **2 Tennessee coneflower** (*Echinacea tennesseensis*), Zones 3–9

K. **2 Prairie coneflower** (*Ratibida pinnata*), Zones 3–10

L. **5 Angelina sedum** (*Sedum rupestre* 'Angelina'), Zones 6–9

M. **4 Sunset Cloud sedum** (*Sedum telephium* 'Sunset Cloud'), Zones 4–9

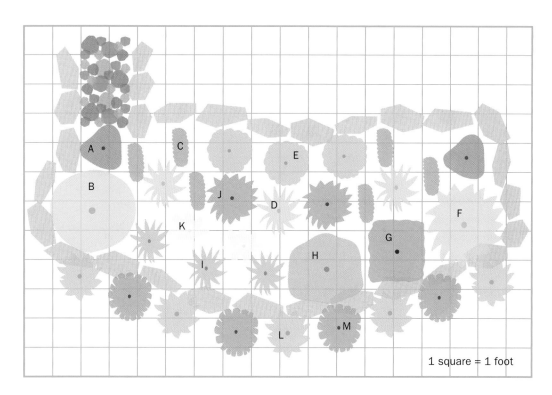

1 square = 1 foot

Don't fertilize

The best rain gardens are made up of a large collection of native plants. These tough plants do not need fertilizer. In fact, excessive nutrients cause natives to grow too tall and flop over. If you are concerned about the nutrient content of your soil, add a 2-inch-thick layer of compost around plants in spring.

Building tips

Percolation test. If you are concerned about the soil's ability to drain where you plan to place the rain garden, conduct a percolation test. Dig a hole below the depth of the proposed rain garden depression. Fill the hole with water. If the water drains away in 12 to 24 hours, the soil drains well and will likely support rain garden plants.

Remove existing vegetation. Any grass or plants growing on the proposed rain garden site must be removed before the rain garden is installed. If you skip this step and don't remove the vegetation, it will continuously pop up in the rain garden and create a weed-filled eyesore. Use a sharp spade to skim away sod or rent a sod cutter from your local home improvement center and get the job done quickly.

Weed, weed, weed. Rain gardens require regular maintenance, especially during the first couple years. Weeding is one of the most important things you can do to keep your rain garden in top form. Right after planting, spread a 2- to 3-inch layer of shredded hardwood mulch over the area to suppress weeds. Replenish the mulch layer annually. Once a week, take time to pull weeds that break through the mulch layer.

designing & planning

Take some time to thoughtfully consider your landscape and your lifestyle, and then make a water garden plan so you can drink in the joy of a cool oasis in precisely the spot where you'll enjoy it.

p.90

ASSESS YOUR PROJECT

Square footage, slope, soil quality, and a host of other factors will influence your project. Learn what to look for when planning.

p.94

MAKE A PLAN

The best water gardens contribute to your entire landscape, not just one area. Make a plan before you build to ensure your investment reaches its potential.

p.98

CHOOSE A PROFESSIONAL

Installing large ponds and waterfalls is best left to professionals. Check out these tips for choosing the best contractor for your job.

Site considerations

Waterfalls have the most natural appearance when they are incorporated into an existing slope. In this beauty, water courses over three drops before tumbling into the pond.

Just as every gardener has unique interests and talents,

every property presents unique attributes. Take cues from your landscape to gauge which type of water feature might be a good fit for your space. Some features lend themselves more readily to specific types of landscapes. A backyard with a pretty but precarious slope, for example, isn't the ideal site for a pond. But a sloping yard can be a perfect setting for a waterfall.

By working with the inherent features of your landscape instead of against them, you'll be able to save money by avoiding the lofty costs that accompany moving truckloads of soil from one area to another. Invest the money you save in plants, fish, or some cozy pondside seating, and when your project is complete you'll be the owner of a gracious water feature and still have some money in your pocket.

Consider grade and lot size

The topography of your landscape is one of the most significant aspects of the space when it comes to designing a water garden. Ponds are easiest to build on flat ground, while a stream will flow down even a slight slope, 1 foot of fall for every 10 foot of run, for example. A slope that is greater than 1 to 10 will create a quickly moving stream. A depression beside a driveway could be an ideal spot for a dry creek or a stream.

While it might seem logical to position a pond in a depression or low spot that regularly collects water, it is not a good idea. The pond will be overwhelmed with water after a rain, disrupting the ecology of the site. Debris is likely to flow into the pond, and fish and plants will flow out, if the pond is the recipient of too much runoff.

Just as topography steers you toward one feature or another, the size of your lot will do the same. A tiny courtyard will be overwhelmed by a waterfall, but a fountain is likely a good compromise, offering the soothing sound of running water but not blanketing the entire space with stones and waterfall features.

Landscapes that are a quarter acre or larger offer a wealth of water garden options. Link a pond and a fountain or a stream and a waterfall and enjoy multiple water features in one space.

Pet and wildlife particulars

Pets and water gardens can coexist with ease. A new water garden will make a splash with your pet at first, but then it will quickly become just another part of their landscape. A dog that likes to swim does not pair well with a pond but can be trained to stay out of the feature. The same goes for a cat with a penchant for fishing.

Count on your water feature becoming an oasis for neighborhood wildlife. From songbirds and turkeys to raccoons and deer, your water feature will be a stopping place for many animals and provide a great place for you to see wildlife up close.

TEST GARDEN TIP

Water lilies love light

Water lilies and many other blooming water garden plants require at least eight hours of direct sunlight per day to produce and unfurl their breathtaking blossoms. For a pond full of colorful plants, choose a site that gives plenty of sunlight. If your site is short on sunlight, amplify the available rays by trimming nearby trees, if possible.

Your site, your water feature

NEARLY FLAT SITE
Your site is ideal for a pond or bog garden. If the site receives plenty of sunlight, you can easily grow a flower-filled water garden. Shaded sites will host a variety of texture-rich foliage. A freestanding fountain is another good option.

SLOPING SITE
Streams and waterfalls are good partners for sloping landscapes. The steeper the slope, the faster the water will flow. Slightly sloping landscapes, those that drop less than 1 foot for every 10 feet of run, are also ideal for a rain garden or dry creek.

SMALL SPACES
Container water gardens are perfect for patios, balconies, and courtyards where space is a primary design consideration. Ranging from tabletop gardens to large tubs, container gardens will fit in any small garden space.

Building & maintenance

Vigorous water plants, like the ruffled-leaf water lettuce in this large trough garden, must be thinned a couple times a year.

Part of the charm of a water garden is its dynamic nature.

As the water ebbs and flows in your pond or stream, the water quality changes, plants grow or slowly fade away, and a bevy of wildlife may take a dip in the oasis. In response to these natural fluctuations, you will spend time caring for the feature to promote a healthy ecosystem that adds beauty to the landscape.

Just how much maintenance time do water features require? It depends on the type of water garden. Maintenance estimates for common types of water gardens are shown below.

While ponds and streams require more maintenance time than a perennial border, for example, the rewards are worth it. Perennial gardens can't offer the soothing sound of water gliding over and around stones, nor do they host the diversity of wildlife that is possible in a pond. Match your lifestyle and available time with the right water garden and you'll add to the beauty and joy of your outdoor living space.

Water gardens with fish call for a greater investment of time. Plan to spend at least 10 minutes a day feeding fish and watching their movements. Many pest and disease problems can be prevented when you know the habits and routines of your aquatic life. When they deviate from their habits, you'll know something is amiss.

Construction time

In addition to time spent maintaining your water garden, consider the time it will take to install a feature. A tabletop water garden requires a mere 30-minute investment of time to construct, but a roving stream and pond combination can demand upward of 30 days to build.

Rain gardens, small ponds, small streams, bogs, and dry creeks can be installed by two people working together for a weekend if major excavation is not required. You can easily build a container garden or a simple inground fountain in an afternoon.

Above: **The only upkeep this patioside fountain requires is daily topping off with water to replace that lost by evaporation.**

Water garden maintenance

Are you thinking about adding a pond to your backyard? Or maybe you're ready to build a fountain on your patio? Check out this maintenance summary and you'll have a good idea of how much time you'll spend caring for your new feature.

20 MINUTES A WEEK
container garden
rain garden
bog
dry creek

20 MINUTES THREE TIMES A WEEK
small pond

5 MINUTES A DAY
fountain

10 MINUTES A DAY
small stream or waterfall

20 MINUTES A DAY
large pond, waterfall, or stream, or any pond with fish

Make a master plan

Many of the best landscapes, those that complement their surroundings and the lifestyle of the people who enjoy them, begin with a well-thought-out plan. When the requirements of labor and money are substantial, as they are when installing large water features, some time spent planning will pay dividends in the end.

A great way to get started planning is to create a master plan for your property. A master plan is an overview of the site. Think of a master plan as an opportunity to record all your wishes for your landscape on paper along with the permanent features of your space, such as the location of your home, utilities, and mature trees.

When you craft a master plan that involves a water garden, keep the following ideas in mind, integrating them when and where you can. Remember your master plan is not fixed. Just like a water garden, it is dynamic and will change as you learn more about your site and the outdoor living experience you want to create.

Integrate the water feature into your living area. Capitalize on the benefits of your fountain, pond, or stream by integrating it into the area of your landscape where you spend the most time.

Above: **A garden destination in a dry landscape, this graceful fountain provides a welcome respite from heat and dryness.**

Opposite: **Built at the bottom of frequently used steps, this simple rock fountain is in the heart of the landscape.**

Build a fountain near your entryway so you can admire it every time you come and go. Craft a trickling stream alongside your patio and listen to its pleasant sound as you dine alfresco. You'll quickly find that water features add pleasing depth to your outdoor space. You'll soon find yourself retreating to your streamside seating for respite instead of the couch in the living room!

Consider views. A water garden will play a prominent role in your outdoor living space and if thoughtfully placed it will also become an integral part of your kitchen, living room, and other indoor spaces. Place a waterfall or fountain within the view of favorite window and it will serve as an attractive focal point.

In addition to views, take sound into account when adding a waterfall or stream to your master plan. When a water feature is only 10 to 15 feet away from your house, the murmur of flowing water will drift in through the windows.

Keep safety at the forefront. Ponds, waterfalls, and streams all present safety concerns for small children. If you have a toddler in your family, you might want to delay construction of the water feature. Meanwhile, install a large sandbox, and convert it into a pond or bog garden later. Consider installing a fence around the feature; some municipalities require a fence and childproof gate around a water garden.

Allow for access. Situate your water garden where you can reach it from all sides. Existing landscape features such as fences, utility sheds, and other structures can interfere with easy access when you are building and maintaining ponds and streams. Dry creeks and rain gardens are more forgiving of limited access because they require less maintenance.

TEST
GARDEN
TIP
Nifty outline

If you are having trouble visualizing the size and shape of your water garden, grab a garden hose or two and mark the edges of your water feature. A hose is easy to manipulate—curl or stretch it until the shape is just right. Leave the garden hose outline in place for a few days and ponder the potential feature from all angles. It is much easier to amend the size and shape of your feature now rather than after you spent hours excavating the site.

Prepare to build

Small water features can be installed

nearly year-round, but large, complex water features require some advance planning for beautiful, long-lasting results. The weather, season of the year, and other factors will have an impact on installation of large ponds, waterfalls, and streams. Make plans to work with these factors for a seamless building process that results in a well-constructed, enduring water garden.

Late spring is the best time to install a water garden. Snowmelt and frost are gone by this time, and the soil in many locations is relatively dry. Spring is a great time for establishing new plants in and around your water feature. The plants will readily send out new roots in the cool soil and absorb spring and early summer rains, making a strong start before the heat of summer sets in.

In cold-weather areas, if your water garden plan calls for extensive excavation, consider tackling the dirt work in fall and installing the pond, waterfall, or stream during the following spring. Any loose soil in the newly sculpted pond or streambed will settle during the freeze and thaw cycles in fall and winter. Then you can safely assume that your pond is indeed level and your streambed is at the slope you desire.

Above: **Small waterfalls, like this one, and ponds requiring minimal excavation can be dug, lined, and edged in a weekend. Allow the soil in larger features to settle for several weeks before finishing the project.**

Building water features usually requires some soil movement. Dry soil is easier to dig and move than moist or waterlogged soil. Keep an eye on the forecast when you are planning to build your water garden, and dig during a a stretch of time when clear, dry weather is expected.

Ready, set, grow

A special event to be held at your home—like a graduation party or anniversary celebration—often serves as inspiration to embark on home improvement or landscaping projects. If you're imagining that a new water feature would be a hit at an upcoming alfresco party, keep in mind that water gardens take time to mature. For the first few months after installation, a new water feature often looks a little sparse. It's wise to give the garden at least six months to allow plants to fill in bare spots and smooth the edges between the water and the surrounding landscape.

One way to give your garden an always-been-there look from the time of installation is to start with large plants. Instead of planting 4-inch pots of perennials, opt for quart-size plants. Instead of installing container-grown shrubs, go for balled-and-burlapped specimens from a reputable nursery. Of course, the final cost of your project will be greater if you opt to start with larger plants.

TEST
GARDEN
TIP

Holding pattern

When delays prevent planting your water garden, give your plants attentive care to keep them healthy.

One week or less If you'll plant in less than a week, place shade or sun plants in a shaded spot, arranging them so air can freely circulate between plants. Water when the soil is dry. On windy days, check the soil twice; water as needed.

More than a week If you won't plant for a week or more, treat shade plants as above. For sun lovers, give them a spot that receives at least four hours of sun daily. Water when soil is dry.

Left: **Avoid excavating right after a heavy rain. Waterlogged soil is considerably heavier than dry soil and is frustratingly sticky.**

Below: **Placing the edging material is a finishing touch on most features. You'll likely rearrange the stones around the edge of your pond several times to create the perfect natural appearance.**

Choose a professional

When installing a poured concrete water feature, plan to work closely with the contractor to create the look you desire.

Grand waterfalls and long, meandering streams

Grand waterfalls and long, meandering streams are often more than a homeowner armed with a selection of heavy-duty shovels and a small garden tractor can tackle. When your oasis grows into a bigger project than you can manage on your own, call on a professional landscaper for help.

Depending on where you live, there may be companies or individuals who specialize in installing and maintaining water gardens. These experts often have advanced training and excellent experience with soil and weather conditions in your region, making for an efficient installation. For a directory of water garden professionals, check with your state nursery or landscape association or inquire at your favorite local garden center.

Large projects often begin with the help of a landscape architect. Familiar with local regulations, a skilled landscape architect will create a master plan for your space that takes into account essential topography and a comprehensive plan for your water feature.

Meet and greet

Invest time in finding the right professional for your landscape. The two of you will be working together closely throughout the project, so a good relationship is key.

Visit previous projects. Ask potential contractors for a short list of previous projects and then visit those sites, talk with the homeowners, and learn about how the project came together. Inquire whether the work was completed for the estimated price. Talk about what the site looked like at project completion.

Was it neat and tidy or were extra stones, plants, and debris left on site?

Request a written estimate. After finding a landscape professional who appears to be a good match for you and your project, ask for a written estimate of the project. The estimate should cover the project in detail including quantity and amount of stone; specifics on the pumps, liners, and other water garden products; and the sizes and varieties of plants.

Hash out a project timeline. Weather can toss the best-laid plans into the wind, but a reasonable timeline agreed to at the beginning of the project will help keep your expectations on track and your project at the forefront of the landscaper's job list.

Below: **Moving the massive boulders used to create this waterfall and pond combo required the services of a professional.**

Trim the budget

Trim the budget Large water features are a significant investment. Reduce costs with these money-saving tips.

Do the planting yourself. Adding perennials and small shrubs to the perimeter of your water feature can be one of the most rewarding parts of the project. If you enjoy this sort thing, hire the landscaper to install the water feature, but then hire yourself to do the planting.

Shop locally. Enjoy the benefits of limited shipping costs when you use locally quarried stone for your water garden project. This is not an option for all locales because some stone cannot stand up to the rigors of being constantly exposed to water. Investigate local stone options in your area and take advantage of the cost savings.

materials & equipment

Water gardens ebb and flow thanks to a well-chosen combination of materials and equipment. Learn all about liners, pumps, and other water garden essentials for creating an inviting outdoor retreat.

p.**102**
LINERS

A good liner is the foundation of a water garden. Learn about the different types and determine which one is best for your garden.

p.**106**
PUMPS

Power your pond, waterfall, or fountain with a pump. These hardworking devices move water from one area to another and help keep your feature clean.

p.**110**
FOUNTAINS

From tiny bubblers to majestic geysers, there is a fountain for every garden. Read about various types and choose your favorite.

p.**112**
SMALL EQUIPMENT

Although it's not very glamorous, the equipment that helps a water feature function properly is essential support for a success.

p.**116**
ELECTRICAL EQUIPMENT

Safely deliver power to your pumps, lights, and other water garden features with these quick tips.

p.**120**
FINISHING ELEMENTS

Finish a water feature in style with stone, wood, grass, or other edging material. Also consider paths, seating, and garden art.

Flexible liners

Flexible liner is the best
choice for large ponds
and streams. Join
multiple pieces of liner
material with easy-to-use
liner sealant.

Pond liners make it possible to craft a pond, stream, or waterfall

anywhere you please. These nifty pieces of plastic are the ticket to keeping water from sinking into the soil and turning your stream into a dry creek.

There are two types of pond liners—flexible and preformed. We'll dive into the particulars of flexible liners here. Turn the page to learn more about preformed liners.

Flexible liners are made of thick, black plastic that is easy to meld to the shape of your water feature. PVC (polyvinyl chloride) and EPDM (ethylene propylene diene monomer) are the most commonly available. Each product has pros and cons, and the product is that is right for one situation might not be the best fit for another.

PVC liners are moderately durable, lasting an average of about 10 years in the landscape. A PVC liner that is out of the water and exposed to sunlight will quickly degrade, lasting only five years or so. PVC is available in 20- to 32-mil thicknesses. When possible, choose the thickest liner available for greatest longevity. A PVC liner is more lightweight than an EPDM liner, making it easier to work with in large ponds or streams.

A PVC liner is also generally less expensive than an EPDM liner.

EPDM liners are generally more durable than their PVC counterparts. Count on an EPDM liner to last about 20 years in the landscape. When the liner is carpeting a large pond or stream, the extended life span of EPDM is a worthwhile investment. Like PVC, EPDM is available in varying thicknesses; 30- to 45-mil liners are common. EPDM liners are more flexible than PVC liners and thus easier to fit to an irregularly shaped pond; they also offer greater resistance to ultraviolet light.

Begin with underlayment

No matter what type of flexible liner you buy, it will be susceptible to puncture. Prevent holes by blanketing the soil with a cushioning material, called underlayment, before laying the liner. Many commercial underlayment products, known as geotextile materials, will help prevent rocks from piercing the liner. Old carpet can also serve as underlayment. A 2- to 3-inch-thick layer of sand can also be used as underlayment.

TEST GARDEN TIP

Pond plastic only!

When buying liner, don't be tempted to buy less expensive black plastic roof liner or swimming pool liner. These liners are often treated with algae inhibitors and other chemicals and will quickly prove toxic to pond plants and wildlife. The packaging for all pond liners should state that the liner is safe for use with plants and fish.

Calculating liner needs.

Flexible liner is most commonly sold in large, precut sheets. Taking a few minutes to calculate exactly how much liner you need for your water feature will save you time—no need to work with and cut a massive sheet of plastic if you need only a small sheet—as well as money.

The calculations are simple. Begin by imagining your water feature as a rectangle, even though it may be round or irregular. Make sure the rectangle includes the outermost points of the feature. Then measure the depth of the feature. Most ponds are about 2 feet deep.

Next determine the liner width by adding the width of the rectangle measured above to two times the depth of the pond and then add 2 feet for overlap at the edges of the feature. The length of liner is determined the same way. Add the length of the rectangle measured above to two times the depth and then add 2 feet, again for overlap.

HERE'S AN EXAMPLE:
A POND FITS INSIDE A 10-FOOT-WIDE BY 12-FOOT-LONG RECTANGLE. THE POND IS 2 FEET DEEP.

Liner width = 10 + (2×2) + 2   Total width = 16 feet
Liner length = 12 + (2×2) + 2   Total length = 18 feet

A 16×18 FOOT LINER WILL COVER THE 10×12 FOOT POND.

Preformed liners

Preformed liners are not only for inground water features—they're handy for lining containers like this wood barrel too.

Quick and easy to install and well suited to small garden ponds

and waterfalls, preformed liners (also called rigid liners) are available in many ready-made sizes and styles. If you are new to water gardening and building a pocket-size pond, a preformed liner is a great way to get started.

Most preformed liners are constructed of rigid black plastic. A small, 5x7-foot preformed liner starts at about $250. A quick search of a home improvement store will reveal a variety of shapes from geometric circular and rectangular ponds to irregular kidney-shape pools.

Standard preformed liners also come in a variety of depths; some include shallow ledges for marginal plants and deep zones where fish can overwinter. Manufacturers also make preformed waterfall units that can be attached to a pond unit to create a waterfall-pond combination.

Preformed liners are more durable than flexible liners and are easier to repair if damaged. Rigid units also have a distinct advantage over flexible liners for aboveground water gardens, which are ideal in areas where stony soil or tree roots prevent or hinder excavation. You can place a preformed liner either entirely aboveground or install it at any depth. Keep in mind that the liner will not support itself; aboveground ponds need a structure built around them.

During installation, make sure the preformed liner is absolutely level and that you backfill nooks and crevices so the plastic won't collapse under the weight of the water. Also, you have to be careful about using heavy edging, such as stone. Some preformed liner edges are convex and the weight of stone will crush them. Other edges are designed to bear weight (check with the supplier), but they must be fully supported with backfill.

TEST GARDEN TIP
Add a cushion

A minimum of 2 inches of soil mixed with sand backfilled under and around the preformed liner will help prevent winter cracking and splitting. Be sure the sand-soil mix or underlayment is absolutely level before putting the liner in place.

Why black?

Most preformed and flexible liners come in black, a fitting color for garden pools for many reasons. Black is natural looking and blends with the algae that tend to cover it after a few months (the algae help the liner resist damage from ultraviolet rays). Black also gives a pool the illusion of depth. When planted with water lilies, marginal plants, and your favorite pondside plants and edged with stone, a water feature with a black liner appears to have no liner at all.

Pumps

A pump and bubbling fountainhead turn a planting urn into a fountain in the center of this small pond.

The glassy surface of a pond is beautiful, but moving water

adds splash and sparkle to the garden. For that, you'll need a pump. Pumps make streams run, fountains spray, ponds drain, and water recirculate to keep waterfalls falling. Pumps also help keep pond water clean by moving it through filters and clarifiers.

Moving water through a water feature once required complicated plumbing. Today, all you need is a pump. Installation isn't complicated; it takes just minutes to assemble.

Submersible pumps are best

There are two types of pumps—submersible and external. Submersible pumps are the better choice for the majority of water garden projects. No matter what type of pump, the mechanism is a simple set of whirling blades that pressurize the water and force it into motion.

Submersible pumps are less expensive and easier to use than external pumps. They sit directly in the water, unlike external pumps, which must be set up out of the water. Submersibles are easy to install, start without priming, and run quietly.

Size matters

The most important consideration when choosing which pump to buy is its size. The critical measure of pump power is the number of gallons of water it will pump per hour to a specific height, called the head.

To determine the size pump you'll need, first calculate the volume of water in the pond (see page 135). As a rule, choose a pump that can move half the total volume in an hour. Next, if the pump will power a fountain, determine the amount of head pressure the pump will need to overcome to recirculate the water. Head pressure is the height difference from the point where the pump draws water to where it pumps it out.

For example, a pond that holds 500 gallons of water and has a waterfall that is 3 feet above the pump intake will need a pump that moves 250 gallons of water per hour rated for a head pressure of at least 3 feet.

When in doubt, buy a more powerful pump. You can restrict water flow with a valve if the pump is too powerful. When shopping for a pump for a stream or waterfall, make sure its head pressure rating is equal to or greater than the height you've planned for your falls.

TEST GARDEN TIP
Pond-friendly pumps

The best pump for a pond is a pump specifically designed for use in a water garden. These pumps are made to operate 24 hours a day at the very best efficiency level. Pond pumps are also better able to withstand the silt, sand, and other debris that make their way into a water garden than are swimming pool or other pumps.

Before you go shopping
You need to know how you plan to use a pump in order to choose the right type and size for the job. Take note of how water will flow into the pump and how much resistance it will meet along the way. To make the right choice, first answer these questions.

USE How will you use the pump? To power a fountain or waterfall? To filter water in a pond?

VOLUME What is the volume of the water feature? This is typically measured in gallons.

HEAD PRESSURE For features where water runs downhill to a pond, how high above the water surface is the point where water discharges in a waterfall? This is commonly measured in feet. If you have any doubt about the exact height, err on the side of greater height than less.

FILTER If you are considering using the pump to power a separate filter, how many gallons per hour (gph) does it take to properly operate the filter? Check the filter manual. It will include a gph recommendation.

FISH Will your water garden include fish? If so, how many and what size? A big fish population will require a biological filter. After deciding on a filter, ask how many gph are needed to operate the biofilter.

FOUNTAIN If your design includes a fountain, how many gph are required to operate the fountain you choose? Check the packaging that came with the fountain. It will include a gph recommendation.

Choosing a pump

It is easy to become overwhelmed by the wide variety of water garden pumps, but it is

important to learn about pump features so you can choose the very best pump for your oasis.

Since a water feature pump runs continuously, choose a pump that is energy efficient. Compare energy efficiency among similarly powerful pumps by comparing the watts, electrical power consumption, and energy efficiency ratings for the units.

Pond A pump in a pond is primarily responsible for circulating water through a filter, which is often included inside the pump. If there are fish in the pond, select a pump that powers a biofilter. To choose a pump for a pond, begin by calculating the volume of water in the pond (see opposite page). The best pump will be able to recirculate 50 to 100 percent of the

Above: **Selecting the best pump for a waterfall involves measuring the width of the spillway. Larger spillways require more powerful pumps.**

volume of water in the pond in an hour. So a pond that holds 500 gallons of water requires a pump that is rated for 250 to 500 gallons per hour (gph).

Fountain Choosing a pump for a fountain requires only one additional piece of information: the head pressure. This is the height to which the pump must push the water so it spills out the top of the fountain. Calculate head pressure by measuring the height from the water intake on the pump to the top of the fountain. To select a pump, use the water volume of your feature combined with the head pressure measurement.

Streams and waterfalls The width of a stream or waterfall combined with the height of the discharge point are necessary to determine the right pump for the feature.

For each foot of spillway in a waterfall or each foot of streambed, you should plan for a pump to move 1,500 to 2,000 gph. For example, power a 2-foot-wide waterfall by a pump that is rated to 3,000 to 4,000 gph or more. Next, take the head pressure into account. Just like calculating the head pressure rating required for a fountain, head pressure for a stream or waterfall is the distance from the water intake point on the pump to the top of the waterfall or stream. A pump that powers a stream that begins 3 feet above the pump intake point has a head pressure rating of 3 feet.

The length between the pump and the top of the stream or waterfall is another complicating factor in choosing a pump. A pump that moves 3,000 gph at a head pressure of 3 feet will perform relatively well if the pump is a few feet from the top of the water feature. It will not pump as vigorously if the water must travel a great distance to reach the top of the feature. When in doubt, buy a more powerful pump.

TEST GARDEN TIP

Quick volume measure

Here's an easy way to calculate the volume of your pond after you've dug and lined it. Jot down the reading on your water meter. Then fill the garden pond and note the new reading. Most meters measure the amount of water used in cubic feet. Multiply by 7.5 to convert cubic feet to gallons.

Calculating volume

The volume of water in your water garden is a key piece of information you will need to choose the proper pump. Here's how to figure the volume of your garden. For all shapes, the dimensions should be stated in feet. First, calculate the area of the water feature, and then multiply the result by the average depth. Finally, multiply that result by 7.5 to determine volume in gallons.

RECTANGLE OR SQUARE Multiply length by width to find the area.

OVAL Measure from the center to the most distant edge, then from the center to the nearest edge. Multiply the first figure by the second and the result by 3.14 to find the area.

CIRCLE Measure the radius (the length in feet from the center to the edge). Multiply the radius by itself and then by 3.14 to find the area.

ABSTRACT, IRREGULAR, AND OBLONG Break abstract and irregular shapes into simpler units (such as circles and rectangles), then calculate the area of each. If that doesn't work, multiply the maximum length by the maximum width to find the pool's area.

For an oblong shape, figure the area by breaking it into a square and two half circles. Calculate the area of the square. Then consider the two half circles as one and calculate its area.

Fountains

A gently splashing fountain is one of the greatest joys of water gardening.

Not only is the beauty of the moving water a valuable addition to the landscape, but also on a quiet night a fountain adds a relaxing background whisper that you can hear while sitting on your porch or deck.

Fountains are a cinch to incorporate into nearly any size or type of water garden. Even a tiny tub garden can host a small bubbling fountain. Powered by pumps, fountains are available in a variety of spray patterns. Multitiered spray patterns have a bold, formal appearance while more natural-looking fountains simply bubble water above the pond surface.

Above: **A small submersible pump connected to a geyser fountainhead creates the perfect splash in this small pond.**

A fountainhead—also called a sprayhead—is often sold separately from the pump. When choosing a fountainhead, first consider the height and width of its spray pattern, although you can often easily adjust both with a valve on the pump. Second, choose the style that fits the appearance of your water feature. A bubbler, for example, looks natural in a small informal water garden tucked into a perennial border or among shrubs. A mushroom or bell fountainhead is striking in a circular formal pool. And a rotating jet adds dazzle to a modern installation.

Pump power required to run a fountainhead varies greatly depending on the size and type of head. Many pond fountains require a pump that will move 200 to 300 gallons of water per hour. The fountainhead manufacturer will list a recommended pump size; always follow the recommendation.

Moving water

The bubbling, swirling action created by a fountainhead, especially geyser-type and bubbler fountains, aerates the water, which is beneficial for fish. Aerated water will contribute to a healthy pond ecosystem that is better able to moderate changes in water quality. While the fish will appreciate the added oxygenation, it's important to consider the needs of plants. Many, including water lilies, don't grow well when water splashes their leaves. They grow best in a pond with an undisturbed surface. If your pond is large enough, you may be able to install a fountain at one end and tend a collection of water lilies at the other end.

Wind can ruin the effect of the moving water of a fountain. Fountains with delicate or tall sprays need some shelter; strong winds distort the pattern, increase evaporation, and deplete the pool. A thoughtfully placed evergreen hedge or a border of dense deciduous shrubs will do the trick.

Above: **An old millstone is the focal point of this bubbling fountain. The tublike reservoir is hidden underground.**

Your perfect fountain

Pair your pond or container garden with a just-right fountain for a finished garden that has the look and sound you desire. This simple guide will help you choose a fountainhead to fit your water feature.

BELL OR MUSHROOM A great choice for formal pools and water features, bell or mushroom fountainheads have a symmetrical appearance and classy feel. Tiny fountainheads can be incorporated into container water gardens.

BUBBLER Easy to add to any size fountain, from large ponds to tabletop water gardens, bubbler fountainheads have a relaxing, natural appearance and sound.

GEYSER Make a big splash with a geyser fountainhead. The height of a geyser is often easy to adjust using a simple valve on the pump.

MULTITIERED SPRAY Striking when used in a stand-alone fountain or a large pond, a multitiered spray fountainhead has a formal look and the potential to generate a very bold sound.

Skimmers and clarifiers

Mechanical filtration is especially important if a pond includes fish. Skimmers and clarifiers help keep chemical levels in check.

Sparkling clear water is the dream of nearly every water gardener.
Debris-free water allows you to gaze into the depths of your pond and watch fish gliding through the water. When algae are under control you don't have to worry about stringy green threads clinging to your hands after you tend water garden plants. Using mechanical devices such as a skimmer helps maintain clear, healthy water in a water garden, as do biological tactics.

Read on to learn about mechanical ways to keep your water feature clean. A small investment in one or more of these pieces of equipment will go a long way toward creating sparkling water.

All about skimmers
A skimmer prevents problems associated with leaves and other debris that fall into your water feature. When too many leaves and other organic debris collect in a pond, they release so much ammonia that the water can become toxic to fish in winter. Ice that forms on the pond surface traps the harmful substances in the water.

A skimmer removes floating matter before it decays and sinks. It helps maintain water quality by increasing the oxygen level as the skimmed water splashes back into the pond.

How skimmers work

A skimmer sits at the edge of a water feature. A pump inside the device works constantly to draw the water into it. Netting within the skimmer traps debris. Water from the skimmer is then pumped to a filter, waterfall, or other location and recirculates back into the pond.

A skimmer works best when installed downwind, allowing prevailing winds to direct leaves and other floating material toward the skimmer. Recirculated water should reenter the pond at the opposite side from the skimmer. You can increase a skimmer's efficiency by locating it opposite a waterfall or stream. The steady current of water entering the pond helps to propel floating debris toward the skimmer.

Using a skimmer can have some negative effects. While collecting unwanted floating debris, the skimmer may also draw in floating plants. In addition, it may suck in fish, especially little ones, and trap frogs and tadpoles. Check it daily and rescue any trapped pond denizens.

All about clarifiers

If you are looking for a surefire way to avoid green water due to algae, you'll find it with a UV clarifier. The device kills suspended algae, bacteria, and other microorganisms as they flow through the clarifier. A UV clarifier promotes fish health by killing fungi and some parasites that attack goldfish and koi.

A clarifier kills beneficial organisms only if they enter the UV chamber. It won't affect the beneficial bacteria that colonize inside a biofilter and on the sides and bottom of the pond. Be sure to include aquatic plants in a water garden that uses a UV clarifier. Otherwise, you'll end up with clear water that's full of nitrites, which can be detrimental to fish.

How clarifiers work

A UV clarifier consists of an ultraviolet bulb inside a quartz-glass tube and PVC housing. A pump forces water through a pipe to the UV unit, which sits outside the pond. The water is irradiated as it passes between the inside of the housing and the outside of the glass tube. The water is then returned directly to the pond.

UV clarifiers are labeled according to their wattage, maximum gph, and recommended pond size range. Their strength varies. If the maximum flow rate for the UV clarifier is exceeded, algae will move past the UV bulb too quickly to be killed. Buy a clarifier with a maximum gph capacity that exceeds the gph of the pump that sends water to it.

TEST GARDEN TIP

Pump and UV clarifier combo

Keep your eye out for pumps that include an imbedded UV clarifier. These all-in-one units make it easy to power a waterfall or fountain while clarifying the water at the same time. As water passes into the pump, it is directed through a UV filter before being pumped back into the water feature. A benefit of this all-in-one technology, besides simplicity, is that the pump and UV clarifier are designed specifically to work together so the gph capacity is maximized.

Left: **A hardworking addition to any water feature, a skimmer prevents leaves, twigs, and other debris from infiltrating the workings of a pump and causing damage. Here, the skimmer filter is being placed around the pump.**

Filters and pipes

When pond water becomes cloudy, filters offer a solution.

Crystal clear ponds and streams in nature are the result of a delicate balance of plant and animal life along with necessary bacteria and fungi and, more often than not, a large body of water. Because residential water features tend to be small, finding the natural equilibrium among the many players in the ecosystem is a tricky task. A filter will reduce the time you spend caring for your oasis so you can dedicate more time to drinking in its beauty.

Nitrogen cycle knowledge

Filters complement the nitrogen cycle, which keeps pond water in balance. The nitrogen cycle works like this: As ammonia accumulates in the water, beneficial bacteria and enzymes break it down into nitrite. Eventually the nitrite becomes nitrate, which is generally harmless to pond creatures and beneficial to plants.

Above: **A series of rigid PVC pipes buried underground delivers water to the top of this meandering stream.**

Nitrate in water is problematic because algae thrive on it. You can limit the amount of nitrate in water by stocking the pond with a smaller number of fish and smaller fish. Stop feeding fish when the water temperature drops below 50°F. Add more plants. Remove plant debris before it builds up on the bottom of the pond. And, just as important, employ a filter to help achieve a balanced system.

Filter fundamentals

There are two types of filters: mechanical and biological. In addition, aquatic plants do an excellent job of filtering harmful substances out of the water. A plant filter is simply an aquatic plant bed, allowing plants to do the work. If you want to make a plant filter, such as a bog, include it as part of the pond construction.

Mechanical filtration involves forcing pond water through porous media (usually filter pads) that catch larger particles. Most mechanical filters are designed to sit on the bottom of the water feature, but some work outside the feature. Look for an all-in-one unit that includes a filter and a pump.

Biological filters, also called biofilters, trap suspended debris in pond water. Nitrifying bacteria and enzymes inside the biofilter remove ammonia and nitrites from the water. An aboveground biological filter is a good choice for most water features. An inground or pressurized biofilter is most commonly used for large ponds, especially ponds with koi.

Choose a filter based on the volume of your water feature (See page 109 for calculating volume). The best filter should be able to recirculate the feature's water volume at least once every two hours. A 1,000-gallon water feature needs a pump and filter that can handle at least 500 gallons of water per hour.

ASK THE GARDEN DOCTOR

I can see some algae in my pond, but it doesn't detract much from my enjoyment of the feature. Is any algae bad?

ANSWER: A small amount of pond algae is part of a healthy ecosystem. To test the balance, put your hand into the water in your pond. Algae are excessive and need controlling if your hand is not visible when it is a foot beneath the water's surface.

Pipes
Moving water to the spillway of a waterfall or the top of a fountain is a breeze when you employ the right piping for the job. Check out these praiseworthy water garden pipes.

RIGID PVC Use Schedule 40 pressure-rated pipe and fittings in your water garden. They are corrosion resistant, lightweight, and inexpensive, but not flexible. Commonly available in white, the PVC can be spray-painted black if it will be visible underwater.

FLEXIBLE TUBING Also known as corrugated plastic, flexible tubing is especially useful because it is easy to bend. It is available in black or white and can be expensive. Do not bury flexible tubing; it will collapse under the weight of soil.

BLACK PLASTIC This semiflexible, inexpensive piping is available in many styles. It can be buried up to 1 foot deep and because it's flexible it requires fewer elbow connectors than rigid PVC. Use it in or out of the water.

Adding power to your water garden

Home to an intriguing collection of lotus, this waterfall is powered by electrical lines hidden underground.

It has never been easier to add power to your landscape.

Although water features don't require power or any mechanical parts to be successful, they certainly benefit from them. A modest amount of electricity will make fountains bubble and streams run, and help keep pond water clear by powering filters and UV clarifiers. Standard household 120-volt alternating current supplies most of the power for today's water features and their accessories.

The first step in adding electrical power to your water garden is to determine the electrical load needed to operate your planned water feature and all of its components. Pumps and other devices are rated by the manufacturer at a certain number of watts. Compare the total number of watts needed to power your water garden to the number of amps a circuit can hold.

Residential circuit breakers are generally either 15-amp (which can handle a continuous load of 1,440 watts) or 20-amp (which can handle 1,920 watts). For the vast majority of residential water features, a 20-amp circuit is sufficient. When in doubt, consult an electrician.

Installation notes

For safety, install a ground fault circuit interrupter (GFCI) in each electrical outlet when you plan to use electricity in or near water. The GFCI senses any electrical contact with water in addition to current overload. If water contact occurs, the GFCI instantly stops the electrical current. If pump wiring, even aboveground, becomes frayed and water touches the power wire, the electricity is cut off. Some municipalities have specific requirements about GFCI installation and location.

If possible, when laying new electrical lines underground, avoid traversing any area with a septic system, paving, a deck, a patio, or an outbuilding. Run the power line through a PVC Schedule 40 pipe buried at least 18 inches deep. At this depth, the line is less likely to be damaged by digging near it. Consider installing an electrical switch in the garage or on a porch to control the lights or other equipment for your water feature.

ASK THE GARDEN DOCTOR

I would like to do my own electrical work for my water garden. How can I learn about regulations and codes?

ANSWER: Before starting any electrical installation, check with your city or county inspector (department of building inspection). Local building codes have particular requirements depending on the climate and soil conditions. For example, your local code may require underground power lines to be encased in conduit buried at a certain depth.

Left: **Make it easy to turn off the power to waterfalls and other features by installing an electrical switch for the feature on a porch or in a garage.**

Easy-to-install landscape lighting adds hours of enjoyment

to your water garden. When the sun sinks behind the hills, a light sensor triggers landscape lighting to flicker on, illuminating streams, waterfalls, ponds, and the pleasing architectural forms of the plants that surround your water feature.

Requiring only a few watts of electricity, compared to traditional interior lighting systems, low-voltage landscape lighting is a low-energy way to increase the use of your outdoor rooms. Or take advantage of the sun's power with a solar-powered lighting systems. Advances in technology have made these once-finicky fixtures powerful light producers.

Create a lighting plan

With a flashlight in hand, begin crafting your lighting plan by taking a stroll around your landscape after dark. Safety is a main concern when selecting lighting for your water feature. Ample pathway lighting will prevent tripping and stumbling that could send a garden visitor careening into your oasis. When in doubt, add more pathway lighting rather than less to ensure safe travels along your walkways.

The amount of light a low-voltage or solar-powered landscape fixture emits is influenced by several factors, including surrounding plant material. When selecting a location for your landscape lighting, be sure to note how it will interact with annuals, perennials, trees, and shrubs planted nearby. Often the best type of light for paths shines downward, casting light directly on the walkway.

After establishing a plan for safety lighting, move on to lighting the artistic parts of your landscape—waterfalls, streams, fountains, and pleasing plants. Spotlights are often the best way to illuminate these landscape focal points. Spotlights are available in various strengths. To avoid lighting your garden excessively, opt for less light instead of more when choosing and locating spotlights.

Choose your lights

Both low-voltage and solar-powered lights have practical application in the home landscape. Low-voltage lights require little time for installation—you can easily light a 20-foot-long path in a hour. Unlike solar-powered lights, which often do not illuminate at dusk following an intensely cloudy or rainy day, you can count on low-voltage lights to shine brightly no matter the weather.

Solar lights are environmentally smart, and most solar lights on the market today will shine for four or more hours when fully charged. In places where lighting is essential for safe travel, choose low-voltage lights. Solar lights can easily power all other areas.

TEST GARDEN TIP

Dig a trench

Low-voltage landscape lighting cables do not have to be buried underground. You can disguise them under a layer of mulch or tuck them between plants, but for safety and longevity, take a few extra minutes to bury the line. Using a sharp spade, dig a narrow, 3-inch-deep trench. Tuck the cable into the trench and cover it with soil.

Left: **Pathway lights like these are available in a multitude of styles at home improvement centers.**

Opposite: **The subtle glow of underwater lights sets a quiet, meditative scene. Underwater lights are especially striking near a waterfall.**

Edging

Stone, brick, and other materials work to bridge

the gap between a shimmering pool of water or a swiftly moving stream and the surrounding landscape. These edging materials, usually one of the last items installed in a water feature, are an important element in the overall look and feel of the garden.

Edgings are functional too. An edging extends the life of a pond liner by protecting it from sun,

which will quickly degrade the flexible plastic material. A slightly raised edge also protects the feature from water runoff from the surrounding landscape. And the right edging can encourage birds and wildlife to access your pond.

After making a plethora of decisions about your feature, choosing the edging can be a daunting chore. Follow these edging material

Above: **A simple bluestone border gives the eye a place to rest while observing this vibrant, plant-filled pond.**

suggestions to be sure your edging selection matches the water garden you desire.

Natural stone and boulders These popular edging materials provide a look that's as natural as the ponds and streams they border. For the most natural look and to potentially save money, visit a local quarry and choose stone that is native to your area.

Natural flagstone, roughly flat stone, is especially useful around the edge of a pond. It is relatively easy to work with and can simply be stacked as needed. Boulders, large stones, and pebbles always look appropriate in and alongside a stream or waterfall. Combine a range of sizes for the most natural appearance. Partially bury large boulders to make them appear as if they have been in place for years.

Cut stone Slate, bluestone, limestone, granite, and marble give a water feature an elegant, polished look. These costly materials are often used for small, geometric features such as a raised pool.

Bricks, pavers, and concrete block Formal pools and water features are complemented by bricks, pavers, and concrete block. These inexpensive manufactured elements are available in a variety of colors and sizes at local home improvement stores. Invest in a few samples and take time to arrange them near your water feature to get an idea of the finished edge they will create.

Note that bricks and pavers may require mortar to stay in place. Concrete block will usually stay in place without mortar.

TEST GARDEN TIP
One-stop shopping

When possible, purchase all of your stone for a landscaping project at once. The color and texture of stone varies slightly depending on when and where it was quarried.

Natural appearances

In nature, woodland streams, prairie ponds, and trickling waterfalls are usually bordered by a mix of plants and stone. Mimic this informal mingling of differing textures to give your water feature a natural appearance. Avoid encircling the water feature with a necklace of rocks. Instead, alternate groups of plants with clusters of boulders and stones.

Easy-care perennials, such as black-eyed susan and coneflower create color and structure around a pond in full sun. Small conifers are another good option. The borders of shaded water gardens are the perfect places to plant hostas, coral bells, and woodland ephemerals such as bleeding heart and wild ginger.

Seating

Cocktails by the water garden is a cinch with a pondside patio outfitted with ample seating.

Water gardens are guaranteed to make you slow down

and drink in the wonders of nature. You're sure to be captivated by dragonflies skimming across the glassy surface of a pond, goldfish gliding through the water, and water lilies unfurling their silky blooms. Your pond isn't complete until you create a few places to comfortably perch and witness these wonders. Chairs, benches, and tables alongside a water garden create an outdoor living room that will be just as popular as its interior counterpart.

Garden seating can be as simple as a grassy knoll, but you're more apt to linger when the seating is a bit more supportive. Select a level, stable site for your seating area. Be sure it offers generous views of the water garden. If a waterfall or fountain is a focal point, it should be within easy view.

Make the seating area accessible after a rain by carpeting it with a 3- to 4-inch-thick layer of mulch or a 2-inch-thick layer of pea gravel. For easy maintenance, prior to spreading the mulch or rock, remove any existing vegetation and cover the area with landscape fabric to prevent future weeds. Top the fabric with mulch or pea gravel to create a fast-draining, quick-to-dry surface that you can easily use just an hour or two after it rains.

Selecting furniture

Garden furniture styles range from contemporary to French country. Garden seating options do not need to be fresh from the manufacturer. Some of the most pleasing are recycled, reclaimed, or reinvented pieces of household furniture or found objects. A vintage flat-topped trunk can make a nifty bench while providing space to store tools.

Nature abounds for seating options too. A slab of limestone supported by a couple stacks of bricks is an instant bench. See the Test Garden Tip for a wood option.

Extend the life of your garden furniture by protecting it from the elements. Wind, rain, and cold temperatures will degrade wood, metal, and resin pieces over time. In cold-winter areas, store furniture in a shed or garage. Coat wood pieces with polyurethane to prevent moisture from seeping into them.

TEST GARDEN TIP
Simple log seat

An old log or stump makes a perfectly pleasing seat alongside a water garden. Especially fitting in woodland settings, these makeshift chairs and benches blend into the surroundings. Prevent the logs or stumps from shifting by burying the bottom 6 inches in the soil.

All-weather furniture

All-weather or outdoor wicker is made from twisted paper or synthetic fibers, which are woven around a frame and coated with a weather-resistant finish. Unlike traditional wood wicker, all-weather wicker can be exposed to moisture and is cleaned by simply spraying off dust and debris with a garden hose every few weeks. All-weather wicker stands up to the elements, although most manufacturers recommend the furniture be protected from prolonged exposure to full sun.

Other long-lasting and low-maintenance furniture materials include rot-resistant woods like teak, cedar, and Australian jarrah along with products made from wrought iron and resin, a durable plastic.

Paths and bridges

TEST GARDEN TIP
Much about mulch

A 3- to 4-inch layer of mulch is an excellent path material in many parts of the landscape, but it doesn't work well near a water feature. Wind and erosion can easily scuffle the mulch into the pond or stream, where it will likely clog filters, fill skimmers, and generally disturb water chemistry. Instead of carpeting pathways with mulch, choose a stone material or grass.

Paths make it possible to get an up-close view of water

features. They pave the way to the water's edge, creating a safe surface for you to travel as you inspect the nuances of your ever-changing water garden. Playing both a functional and aesthetic role in the landscape, paths are an integral part of the overall appearance of your garden.

Before you begin creating paths near your water garden, consider these questions to help you design a practical pathway. Where will the path begin and end? Is it necessary to add small paths off the main path to direct traffic? How will it work to the advantage of the natural terrain— whether relatively flat or gently sloping—and will it drain well?

Path building basics

Stone is one of the best building materials for garden pathways. Stone—in the form of simple, cost-effective stepping-stones or elegant cut stone or loose gravel—is a long-lasting option that offers years of service and is relatively easy to install. Neatly trimmed grass paths are another sensible option. Define the edges of a grassy path with planting beds or a simple stone border, making it easy for guests to traverse their way through the garden.

Wood chips, pine straw, and shredded bark are commonly used throughout the landscape, but they present some drawbacks and should be avoided around a water garden. See the Test Garden Tip for more details.

Base the width of your path on how it will be used. If the path is a main thoroughfare, commonly used by two people walking side-by-side or as a service path for wheelbarrows and

other small landscape equipment, it should be at least 4 feet wide. Narrow paths are fine for people walking single file; paths measuring 14 to 16 inches accommodate most walkers.

For stability, flagstone and cut-stone paths are best laid on top of a gravel and sand base. Excavate 4 to 6 inches of soil. Spread a 1- to 2-inch base of gravel and top it with a 1- to 2-inch layer of sand. Encourage drainage when excavating the soil and laying the base layers by shaping the path to slope gently to one side.

Ensure good drainage on gravel and grass paths by crowning them in the center. Water will flow away from the path, allowing it to dry quickly after rain. To build a gravel path, excavate about 6 inches below the soil surface. Lay a 4-inch layer of road grade gravel or crushed stone. Top it with landscape fabric and spread a 2-inch layer of pea gravel over the top.

Span the water

Cross from one side of your water feature to the other on a bridge. These functional landscape elements become focal points when eyecatching materials and striking designs are used. Bridges can be installed after a water garden is constructed, but it is often easier and more cost-effective to build a bridge as you are building your water feature.

Use stone to create a simple bridge across a stream garden. Large stepping-stones placed 8 to 12 inches apart across the center of the stream make for easy crossing and present a sense of adventure at the same time. Be sure to choose stones that extend at least 2 inches above the water surface.

Above left: **A neat and tidy gravel path rings this water lily pond. The simplicity of the path complements the landscape's formal design.**

Above right: **Make it easy to get a close look at a water garden with generous stone steps like these. The rugged stone slabs blend well with the boulders around the pond.**

Opposite: **A slight arch in the design of this bridge makes it both a functional pathway and a pretty water garden focal point.**

Art in the garden

Water gardens are works of art. The mirrorlike surface of a shimmering pond reflects nature's art, showcasing everything from the delicate blossoms of pondside plantings to pretty cloud patterns overhead. Water gardens offer so much beauty themselves that it can be challenging to enhance them further, but a just-right piece of art or thoughtful planting combination can amplify the beauty of your water garden.

Use the following ideas as a guide to ornamenting your pool, stream, waterfall, or fountain. There are no right or wrong ways to add art to the landscape; if you love a particular piece, then it deserves space in your garden and it will contribute to your beautiful setting.

Above: **A sculpted fountain sends water cascading into a shallow pool filled with parrot's feather.**

Opposite above: **While live herons are often a nuisance in a water garden, especially those that are home to fish, these beauties will not cause any harm.**

Art in the garden

Choose objects with meaning. Garden art that tells a story brings instant authenticity to a space. A piece of statuary from your grandmother's garden will have a much greater impact than a piece plucked off the shelf of a mass merchant. Not only will you appreciate the story behind your garden art, but you'll also be able to share the joy with garden visitors.

Art does not have to be old to tell a story. It might be a piece that you picked up while traveling that conjures up fond memories. Or perhaps it is the craft of a dear friend or beloved artist.

Plants are art too. The way you group annuals, perennials, and shrubs transforms them from individual plants to artistic compositions, especially when the combination is reflected in a water garden. Pay close attention to color, line, and texture when composing plantings in and around your water garden.

Fountains offer many options. Instead of a bell or bubbler fountainhead, use simple plumbing techniques to pump water through a piece of statuary, a glazed urn, or a unique found object.

Placement is important. Garden art does not require prominent placement in the garden. A slightly hidden location often offers more drama and intrigue. Tuck a small sculpture among the leaves of hostas in the shade garden where it has the potential to be discovered instead of showcased. Curving walkways and out-of-the-way nooks offer additional areas for visitors to discover art.

Embrace the artistic qualities of garden furniture. A bench crafted of driftwood or a table adorned with colorful pieces of cast-off tile add just as much interest to the garden as a piece of sculpture. Make your garden furniture multitask by choosing pieces that are just as eye-pleasing as they are functional.

Winter care for garden ornaments

Prolonged exposure to sleet, snow, and cold temperatures will quickly shorten the life of many materials. Protect garden ornaments from the elements by moving them to a protected location when temperatures regularly fall below freezing. An unheated garage or shed works well.

If an item is too heavy to move, cover it with a heavy tarp secured with twine. Choose an earthtone tarp so it blends into the landscape. Be sure to remove pumps and filters from fountains and drain plumbing to prevent damage caused by water freezing inside the equipment.

building water gardens

Gather all the know-how you need to craft your own stream, pond, or container water garden from the following pages. They are packed with step-by-step instructions and timesaving ideas.

p.130
PONDS AND POOLS

Check out these easy ideas for building a mini pond in a weekend. Planning a bigger pool? Simply apply these tips to your feature.

p.136
STREAMS AND DRY CREEKS

Learn how to quickly channel water through your backyard with a stream or dry creek.

p.138
WATERFALLS

Discover how easy it is to add water music to your backyard oasis with these building tips. Enjoy a gentle splash or a bold cascade—the choice is yours!

p.142
FOUNTAINS

Some of the smallest fountains require an hour or two to assemble. Learn all about basic fountain components.

p.144
RAIN GARDENS

You'll be surprised at how plants will flourish in your rain garden. Set aside a few minutes each week to keep perennials in top shape!

p.148
BOGS

Bogs are a source of nourishment for a host of nature's critters. Be sure to make your bog garden wildlife-friendly.

p.150
CONTAINERS

A watertight container is all you need to host a water garden on your patio, balcony, or porch. Add plants and enjoy!

Build an inground pond

Whether you dream of a water lily pond or a watering hole for
wildlife, an inground water garden is an asset to almost every landscape. A small inground pond that has a surface area of about 100 square feet or less is a good do-it-yourself project. (Larger projects are best excavated by a backhoe and then constructed by a professional.)

Begin by gathering your tools. You'll need a sharp spade, a wheelbarrow for hauling dirt, a garden hose for marking the shape of the pond, stakes and garden twine, a straight 2×4 to span the width of the pond, and a carpenter's level.

Dig in

Excavation of even a small water garden is often the most taxing part of the project. Smart digging will transform the project from frustrating to fun. Invite a friend to help out and allow plenty of time to excavate your pond. Make sure your tools are well suited to the task, and take time to sharpen your spade before you begin to dig.

Start by marking the outline of the pond with a garden hose. Finetune the outline with stakes (every foot or so) and twine. Cut along the

Above: **In cold regions, build a pond that is at least 3 feet deep to ensure fish can safely overwinter in the feature.**

Opposite: **Excavate a pond after a light rain. It is easy to sink a spade into slightly moist soil, yet the soil will be light enough that it is easy to move.**

outline with a spade, and then remove the top layer of sod. If you plan to edge the pond with stones or other material, dig an outward-sloping shelf (6 to 8 inches wide and about 2 inches deep) beyond the pond edge for the liner and the edging material. The shelf should be deep enough for the edging stones to sit flush with the surrounding soil.

Next, mark the outlines for marginal shelves within the pond; then begin digging from the center outward. As you dig, angle the sides slightly, about 20 degrees from vertical and make sure the edges of the pond are level; otherwise the liner will show. With a small project, you can place a carpenter's level on a straight 2×4 to check all around the pond. For a larger project, place a stake in the middle of the pond with its top at the planned water level. Rest one end of a long, straight board on the stake and the other end on the edge of the pool. Carefully check the level. Rotate the board a few feet, again noting the level.

Next spread the underlayment and top it with the liner. If you are using a flexible liner, take time to fold where needed so it fits the pond.

TEST GARDEN TIP

Save soil

When digging a pond, keep good-quality topsoil, which you can reuse, and poor-quality subsoil, which you should discard, separate by tossing them into different wheelbarrows or onto different tarps.

Anatomy of an inground pond

While inground ponds are as unique as the gardeners who create them, every watering hole includes a few basic elements that function together to create a sparkling pond that is friendly to plants and wildlife.

ESSENTIAL ELEMENTS
Pond liner
Underlayment
Edging material
Pump and filter (optional)

Marginal shelf

Marginal plants

Edging

Liner

Underlayment

Water lily

Simple inground pond

You can build a small garden pond in a weekend.

Make the best use of your time by organizing your tools and materials beforehand. You can make quick work of purchasing supplies by visiting a home improvement store for a pond liner, edging materials, pump (if desired), and pond plants. You'll likely find a large selection of products for a variety of sizes and styles of water features. Another excellent place to shop is a local garden center that specializes in water gardening. Hold off on purchasing fish. Wait a few weeks to allow beneficial bacteria to take up residence, then add fish.

Above: **Measuring about 3 feet wide, a small pond like this one is perfect for a small yard or entryway.**

Inground pond building tips

If you're new to water gardening, using a preformed liner like the one below is a perfect way to line your first garden pond. Easy to install and durable, preformed liners are available in a variety of sizes and shapes at your local home improvement center.

MATERIALS LIST
Pond liner
Underlayment
Edging material
Pump and filter (optional)

1 OUTLINE IT
Using a garden hose, outline the shape of your pond. Look at it from several angles, adjusting the hose as needed to achieve the look you want.

2 ADD UNDERLAYMENT
After using a sharp spade to excavate the pond, add and smooth the underlayment. A 2-inch layer of sand is used as underlayment here. You can also use a purchased textile product as underlayment.

3 POSITION THE LINER
It is essential that the pond liner be level. Using a straight 2×4 and a carpenter's level, check the level of the pond in several directions. Remove the liner if necessary and add or remove sand underlayment until the liner is level.

4 PLACE EDGING
Use stone, brick, or wood to cover the edge of the pond liner. Be sure the plastic lip of a preformed liner is supported by slightly packed soil before placing a weighty stone edging.

5 FILL THE POND
Tap water is perfect for a garden pond. If your pond will include fish and other critters, be sure to treat the water for chlorine and chloramine before adding the aquatic creatures.

6 ADD PLANTS
Finish the pond by adding a variety of aquatic plants. Place marginal plants on the shallow shelves around the edge of the pond and reserve deep regions for water lilies and lotuses.

Create an
aboveground pool

Positioned on the edge of
a patio and planted with
lofty taro and water iris,
this aboveground water
garden becomes a pretty
living fence.

Aboveground pools and ponds are a great way to garden where

digging is difficult, and they're also appealing because they bring the water up close, which is especially enjoyable near a patio or other sitting area.

Raised water features tend to take longer than sunken ones to build and usually cost more. However they require less maintenance after installation because they are less likely to become cluttered with blowing leaves and eroding soil.

Building tips

Aboveground pools must be built from materials sturdy enough to withstand the outward pressure of water. Brick or concrete block veneered with stucco, brick, tile, or stone are popular. Stacked wood timbers are another possibility. The timber structure is lined with a preformed pond liner.

The height of an aboveground pool can vary from 1 foot to much taller. For a pool that's completely aboveground, the ideal height is between 24 and 30 inches, so visitors can easily see fish or sit on the edge of the feature. A pool should be at least 18 inches deep to ensure it is insulated against the elements. For a pool that rises aboveground less than that height, partially excavate it to give it the required depth.

Wooden raised pools are simple to make; masonry projects require more time and skill. Structures made of wood are most successful when constructed from pressure-treated lumber or aged redwood to prevent rot. A masonry aboveground pool will need a concrete footing around the perimeter of its base. The depth of the footing depends on your climate; check local codes for proper depth.

Aboveground pool building tips

If possible, build your aboveground water feature where you plan to place it. This will eliminate the chance that the constructed pool doesn't fit through a narrow door or gate. Building in place also eliminates the cumbersome chore of transporting the bulky project.

MATERIALS LIST
Preformed or flexible liner
Underlayment
Exterior material—brick, wood, and concrete block are common
Pump and filter (optional)

1 PLACE THE LINER
Preformed liners are especially useful for aboveground features. Here, a rectangular preformed liner is supported by a sturdy wood box. Casters on the bottom of the box make it easy to move.

2 SECURE THE LINER
Although preformed liners are rigid, when filled with water they will collapse if not supported. Securely attach the liner to the support structure with screws or nails.

3 FINISH WITH A FRAME
Finish an aboveground pond in style by masking the liner. A wood frame that matches the rest of the structure is used here. Stone or brick will also work well.

4 ADD PLANTS
Aquatic plants thrive in an aboveground pond during warm months. Winter is challenging in cold climates, as the exposed pond will likely freeze completely. Overwinter plants indoors.

Constructing streams and dry creeks

Carefully constructed to resemble a natural woodland stream, this bubbling backyard watercourse is edged with partially buried boulders and decaying logs.

Good news—an existing slope is not required to make streams and dry creeks flow.

You can mold your own moving waterway by using excavated soil from the terminus of the stream or dry creek to build up the starting point of the feature. The greater the slope, the faster the water will move and the more sound it will make.

Streams flow into a pond or stone-filled reservoir. Water pools here before it is pumped to the top of the stream for recirculation. The reservoir should hold twice the volume of the stream. Determine the necessary size of your reservoir by first calculating the volume of the stream (see page 109 for calculating volume). Use the volume of the stream to calculate the length, width, and depth of the reservoir. If the stream holds 100 gallons of water, the volume of the reservoir (result of multiplying its length by width by depth) should be at least 200 gallons.

While streams are time-consuming to build, dry creeks come together quickly. After excavation, you simply line the watercourse with landscape fabric and top it with a variety of stones. Bring your dry creek to life by adding plants along the edges and in the path of the creek as well. Be sure to choose sturdy perennials and small shrubs for planting in the creek so they'll stand strong during an occassional rush of runoff.

ASK THE GARDEN DOCTOR

How do I make my stream look like it has been around for years?

ANSWER: To add instant age to your stream, start by edging it with stones in a variety of sizes. Place a few medium-size boulders along the edge, partially burying them so they look rooted in the landscape. Then add 3- to 4-inch river rock in large swaths and finally fill in empty areas with 1- to 2-inch river rock.

A small bog or two along the side of the stream will also give it a long-established look. A bog near the reservoir at the end of the stream is another popular choice.

Stream and dry creek building tips

When choosing a location for your stream or dry creek, be sure to select a spot that is accessible at all points. Moving water draws attention, and you'll relish the experience of walking along the bank of the stream or dry creek*.

MATERIALS LIST
Flexible pond liner
Underlayment
Liner sealant
Pump and tubing
Skimmer (optional)
Edging material
Stones

Dry creeks require landscape fabric and stones.

1 DON'T FORGET A RESERVOIR
A common mistake in creating a stream is not building a large reservoir at the end of the course. The reservoir should hold twice the volume of the stream.

2 DIG SMART
Begin excavating in the center of your stream or dry creek. This will be the deepest part of your water feature. Gradually slope the sides; be sure the sides are level when you finish.

3 EXTEND THE LINER
Ensure water doesn't flow out of your stream by extending the liner 1 foot or so beyond the edging material. Cover the exposed liner with additional edging.

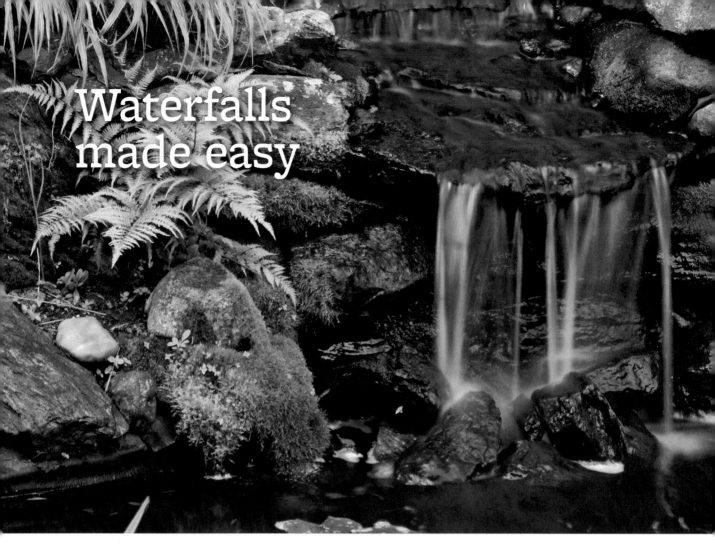

Waterfalls made easy

A waterfall is one of the most challenging

water gardening projects to install, but it is also one of the most rewarding. If a waterfall is your first foray into the world of water gardening, start small so you can learn the basics of building these cascading treasures before making a large investment in the stones, plumbing, and time required for a grand waterfall.

Waterproofing is an essential part of constructing most water gardens, but it is especially important when designing and building a waterfall. Working with a combination of stone and a sloping site leads to a host of potential crevices and low spots where water can flow out of the watercourse and thwart your efforts to create a watertight water garden.

Preformed waterfall liners are made of plastic or fiberglass. They are easy for first-time water gardeners to install and significantly reduce the chances of water flowing out of the watercourse. Installation is straightforward when you follow the manufacturer's guidelines for building the proper base for the waterfall and choosing a pump to power it.

Natural favorite

Although the looks of preformed waterfalls have improved significantly over the years, the most popular waterfalls continue to be those edged with natural stones. Most watercourses involve a flow of water between an upper basin, or header pool, and a lower, larger reservoir.

Multiple-cascade waterfalls (those with a series of waterfalls in a stream) should have a basin of water to supply each cascade, starting with the smallest basin at the top and ending with the largest pool. Vary the length of the basins and the height of the falls for the most natural-looking waterfall.

Make each basin level across its width, and make the overflow area 1 or 2 inches lower than the upper edge of the basin. Be sure to thoroughly tamp the excavated soil. If the ground were to settle, the basin's edge and liner could become uneven and cause water loss. Form an elevated ledge or berm of earth around the perimeter of the excavation to avoid water loss and to keep out unwanted surface runoff.

Above: **The size, shape, and placement of the spillway affects the sound of a waterfall. Instead of spilling directly into the reservoir, this waterfall cascades onto small boulders, creating a different sound.**

Opposite: **It's essential to fully support preformed liners with soil. Take time to carefully pack soil under the liner edge.**

Water music

Tuning your waterfall is part of the joy of creating it. The most noticeable sound is usually generated at the falls, but the watercourse is also a source. The amount and rate of water flowing over the falls determines the quality of the sound, as do the stones within the falls. Even slight movement of the stones within the falls will cause the water to cascade over the surface and splash into the pond below with a different tune. Within the stream you can slow fast-moving water, causing it to bubble and ripple, by placing a few medium stones in the center of the stream to disrupt the flow.

Anatomy of a waterfall

Stones form the bones, or structure, of a great waterfall. Unlike ponds that host a large collection of flowers and foliage, waterfalls are ripe with stones of various shapes and sizes. How and where you place stones will create the look and feel of your feature. In addition to stones, a waterfall contains the following essentials.

ESSENTIAL ELEMENTS
Liner
Underlayment
Pump and tubing
Stones

Basin

Cascade

Pump

Flexible liner

Underlayment

Flexible tubing

Tips for building waterfalls

Moving water packs a punch.

It can dislodge surprisingly large stones. Anchor stones in your watercourse with an easy-to-use product called waterfall foam, which is available at home improvement stores. Great for small and medium stones, waterfall foam works like glue to keep stones in place. It is also commonly used to make a water-resistant seal. The product expands as it dries and ensures efficient water flow over rocks. It is black and it blends into the liner. Before securing any waterfall stones in place, take time to lay stones along the entire watercourse. View the stonework from several angles and rearrange the rocks to achieve the just-right look.

Above: **A variety of stones—from river rock to boulders—gives this new waterfall an always-been-there look.**

Waterfall building tips

A quality carpenter's level is an essential tool for building a waterfall. The watercourse must be level from side to side as it progresses down the slope. Any low spots will send water running out of the waterway. Check levels frequently to avoid frustrating leaks when you fill the feature with water.

ESSENTIAL ELEMENTS

Flexible pond liner
Underlayment
Stones
Pump and tubing
Skimmer
Liner sealant
Waterfall foam

1 USE A WEIR
Large waterfalls benefit from a device called a weir to direct water. Place a weir at the highest point of the stream and disguise it with small boulders or stones.

2 CONNECT THE TUBING
Black plastic tubing transports water from the reservoir at the bottom of the falls to the weir at the top. Bury the tubing in a trench that is about 6 inches deep.

3 PREPARE THE FALLS
A sharp spade, shovel, and a garden rake are useful for sculpting the falls and retention pond. The greater the grade change, the more sound the water will make as it moves.

4 LEVEL THE SKIMMER
Outfitted with brushes to further clean the water before it enters the pump, the skimmer box must be level so that water can flow into the unit without interruption.

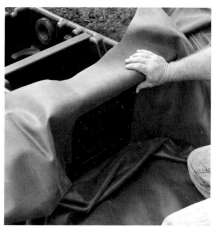

5 SECURE THE LINER
Skimmers and weirs made for large water gardens often include detachable pieces on the pond side of the unit so that the liner can be integrated seamlessly, preventing leaks.

6 GLUE STONES IN PLACE
Waterfall foam prevents stones from toppling down the stream along with the rushing water. It not only holds stones in place but also prevents water from flowing underneath them.

Install a fountain

In the time it takes to watch a movie on the big screen,

you can add the sight and sound of water to your landscape with a fountain. Incredibly easy to install, fountains are available as kits at your local garden center or home improvement center. Or you can buy the pieces individually and build a custom fountain for your deck, patio, pond, or garden bed.

Pump power

A pump supplies the power to a fountain. The fountainhead will determine the size of pump needed. The manufacturer's instructions will provide a recommendation in gallons per hour (gph). If a quality water garden pump is not provided with the fountainhead, purchase one that is within the recommended gph range.

Above: **An underground reservoir captures the water bubbling out of this ball fountain. A pump located in the reservoir propels the water to the top of the fountain.**

Fountainheads are usually connected directly to a submersible pump or to a pipe that is then connected to the pump. A diverter valve may be placed between the pump and fountainhead to adjust the height of the spray.

The fine jets of a fountainhead clog easily. Prevent clogging by installing a mechanical filter that removes particles before they enter the pump. Or use a foam pump protector or foam prefilter, and clean it whenever you notice a lessening of water flow.

Quick and easy setup

Most freestanding fountains come preplumbed, and installation is simple. Check the level of the site on which the fountain will rest, and make necessary adjustments to even it up. Use sand, soil, or stone as needed to level the site.

Then fill the fountain with water and plug it into a GFCI outlet. You can disguise the cord by burying it under the soil surface, but do not bury the connection. Instead, leave it aboveground, wrap it with waterproof tape, and disguise it with stones or set it among plants.

Inpond and out-of-pond fountains with inground reservoirs are only slightly more complicated to install. Again, a level site is key. Take time to ensure the site is perfectly level and stable to prevent problems later on. If you are building your own fountain, don't forget that the base needs to be hollow to allow the pump cord to protrude from the unit.

> **TEST GARDEN TIP**
>
> **Protect the pond liner**
> When you install a pedestal to support a fountain or other large element in your pond, put an extra layer or two of liner under the pedestal base to prevent tears and leaks.

Fountain building tips

A simple underground reservoir is the base of many different types of fountains, including glazed urn fountains, which are popular, and the pretty stone ball fountain on the opposite page. Here's how to set up a reservoir.

MATERIALS LIST
Fountainhead
Pump
Pipe to connect fountainhead and pump*
Flexible liner for reservoir*
Diverter valve*
Required for some fountain projects

1 USE A 5-GALLON BUCKET
A clean 5-gallon bucket makes an effective, inexpensive underground reservoir for small fountains and the pumps that power them. Place the bucket in the ground so it rises about 2 inches above the surrounding soil.

2 COVER THE RESERVOIR
A wire grate and fine mesh screening prevent leaves and other debris from clogging the reservoir. Disguise the barriers with river rock, flagstone, pavers, or boulders.

3 ADD WATER
On windy days, water quickly evaporates from fountains. Top off the water in the reservoir every day or so to prevent damaging the pump when the water level falls too low.

Plant a rain garden

Building a rain garden begins with choosing

the right spot for this environmentally smart feature. Functioning like a catch basin for water flowing out of downspouts or off a driveway or other impermeable surface, a rain garden is best located where water from these surfaces will naturally flow into it.

Many residential rain gardens are situated near the corner of the house, where they capture runoff from the roof and allow it to slowly filter into the soil. To protect the foundation from moisture, locate the rain garden at least 10 feet away from your home. A site 10 to 30 feet away from the foundation is usually just right. If the garden is sited farther than 30 feet, the water will have an excessive path to travel from the downspout to the garden.

Topography is another key consideration when choosing the site. The best site will slope gently away from the home or other impervious surface. A downward slope will ease movement of the water to the garden. A site that slopes 5 percent or less is optimal. A berm installed around the outer edge of the garden will prevent water from flowing away.

A rain garden of any size, even a seemingly small, 50-square-foot patch, will reduce surface runoff and help improve groundwater quality. But build the rain garden as large as possible to make an even greater impact and create space for a diverse collection of plants. Most home landscape rain gardens are 100 to 300 square feet. The larger the garden, the more time and effort required to excavate. If this is your

Above: **Water from the nearby garage roof collects in a rain garden. Native perennials and grasses create an easy-care garden.**

first rain garden, start small, perhaps with a 100-square-foot feature. You can always expand the garden or add another garden nearby.

Carving out the garden

Take cues from the type of soil in your rain garden site when determining the depth of the garden. Sand or loam soils, those that crumble easily when squeezed in your hand, drain faster than clay soils. You know your soil is clayey if you can easily form it into a ball. Fast-draining sand or loam soils call for a 4- to 6-inch-deep rain garden. Gardens in clay soil need to be 6 to 8 inches deep to allow space for water to accumulate and slowly drain into the soil.

Build a 6- to 8-inch-tall berm around the side of the garden opposite from where water enters. The berm will serve as a dike to prevent water

from flowing out of the garden during and after a major rain event. Save the excavated soil and use it to form the berm around your garden. For easy construction, use a wheelbarrow to move the soil from the excavation area directly to where the berm will be constructed.

Build the berm so it has slightly sloping sides. You may want to seed the outward side of the berm with grass, so be sure that the slope you create is easily mowable. You can plant the inward side of the berm with perennial rain garden plants.

As you excavate the garden, work carefully to ensure the garden is level. High and low spots will cause water to pool for long periods, harming the plants. See the Test Garden Tip for checking the level of your garden.

On the level

A level outer edge makes way for a successful rain garden. Ensure that your hard work of digging the rain garden produces near-perfect results by accurately checking the level of the site. When the garden has been dug out and the outer edge appears level to your eye, lay a 2×4 board across the garden and set a carpenter's level on it. Find the spots that aren't level. Fill in the low places and dig out the high spots.

Check the level all around the garden by moving the board in different directions, filling and digging as necessary to make the edge level.

Anatomy of a rain garden

Rain gardens are all about thoughtful soil sculpting. Unlike ponds and waterfalls, rain gardens don't require liners and pumps. They rely on gravity and your attention to detail when excavating.

ESSENTIAL ELEMENTS
Rain garden plants
Topsoil, if garden is built on a significant slope and soil is needed to fill

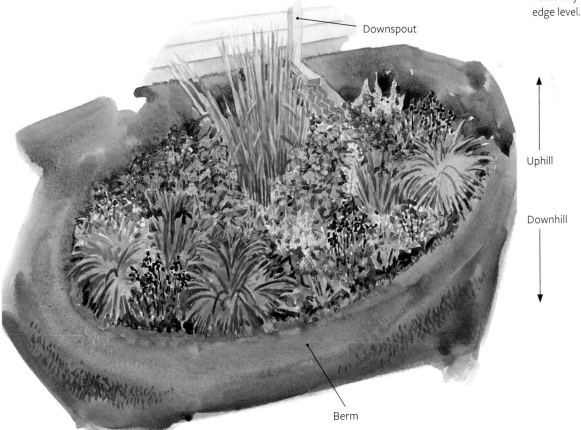

Downspout

Uphill

Downhill

Berm

Building and caring for your rain garden

Rain gardens have received a bad rap recently

for developing a neglected appearance a couple years after planting. Avoid the unkempt look by paying close attention to color, texture, and bloom time of the plants you select for your garden. Due to its proximity to the house, the garden will likely be a focal point in your landscape. Aim to have intriguing interest in every season and a pleasing combination of plant heights year-round. In the garden, arrange plants in clusters of three or five for a colorful impact.

Blanket the garden with a 2-inch-thick layer of wood mulch after planting, and provide at least 1 inch of water a week during the first growing season. The garden will rarely need watering in the second growing season and beyond. Weed the garden as needed, and divide plants in spring if they begin encroaching on nearby plants.

Above: **Keep your rain garden tidy by spending 15 to 20 minutes each week removing spent blooms. Black-eyed susan will bloom for months if it is deadheaded regularly.**

Rain garden plants
For a rain garden that is full of color from spring through fall, include plants that sparkle in each season. Plant in sweeping clusters of three or five plants for pretty swaths of color. Be sure to incorporate small shrubs and trees for interest in winter.

SPRING
American cranberry viburnum (*Viburnum trilobum*)
Columbine (*Aquilegia* spp.), pictured
Louisiana iris (*Iris* spp.)
Pagoda dogwood (*Cornus alternifolia*)
Serviceberry (*Amelanchier laevis*)
Spicebush (*Lindera benzoin*)

SUMMER
Black-eyed susan (*Rudbeckia hirta*)
Joe-pye weed (*Eupatorium maculatum*)
Liatris (*Liatris spicata*), pictured
Purple coneflower (*Echinacea angustifolia*)
Sedge (*Carex* spp.)
Swamp milkweed (*Asclepias incarnata*)
Switch grass (*Panicum virgatum*)

FALL
Big bluestem (*Andropogon gerardii*)
Black-eyed susan (*Rudbeckia hirta*)
Joe-pye weed (*Eupatorium maculatum*), pictured
New England aster (*Aster novae-angliae*)
Sedge (*Carex* spp.)
Snowberry (*Symphoricarpos albus*)
Switch grass (*Panicum virgatum*)

Rain garden building tips
The most taxing part of building a rain garden is excavating the site. Make quick work of the digging by inviting a friend or two to join you. Be sure to ask them to bring along their favorite wheelbarrow and spade so you can quickly move soil.

1 LAYING OUT THE SITE
Be sure to plan for a 6- to 8-inch tall berm along the edge of the rain garden opposite where the water enters the site. The berm for this garden will be on the left.

2 EXCAVATING
Most rain gardens are 4 to 8 inches deep. If the existing soil drains quickly a 4- to 6-inch deep garden is sufficient. Excavate 6 to 8 inches in slow draining soil.

3 BUILDING THE BERM
Transfer soil from the center of the rain garden to the outer edge to form a berm. A gently sloping berm will allow you to mow the yard-side and plant the garden-side.

4 PLANTING
For year-round structure and interest, include moisture-loving shrubs, along with perennials, in your rain garden. Serviceberry and American cranberry viburnum are good options.

5 FINISHING TOUCHES
Adding a 2- to 3-inch-thick layer of organic mulch will help conserve soil moisture and keep weeds at bay. Plan to apply a fresh layer of mulch each spring to prevent weeds.

Easy-care bog gardens

In nature, streams and ponds have wet, boggy areas along their edges.

In garden settings, a bog imitates a marshy place where plants grow in wet, spongy ground. The best location for your bog is a spot that receives at least five hours of direct sunlight a day. Avoid sites with standing water; the drainage in these areas is likely so poor that a bog garden planted there will quickly turn into a swamp. A good bog garden will drain within 24 hours.

Bog garden construction differs from pond construction mainly in terms of depth. A bog is typically 18 to 24 inches deep with sloping sides. Your bog can be as large as you would like. The larger the bog, the wider the range of unique bog garden plants you can grow. Aim for a bog garden that is at least 10 square feet.

After excavating the bog, line it with flexible pond liner. Allow 6 to 8 inches of liner to extend above the soil surface in case the bog settles. About a foot below the soil surface, puncture the pond liner every foot or so around the perimeter of the garden. This allows some drainage, which is necessary for a healthy bog. Perforate the bottom of the liner every 3 feet to further prevent standing water.

Fill the bog with the excavated soil. Enrich the soil with a 2-inch layer of compost if you like. Add plants and then water the soil deeply. Add a 2-inch layer of mulch to help the soil retain moisture and water your bog regularly to ensure the soil never dries out.

Above: **A new bog garden invigorates a once staid patch of lawn with a host of water-loving plants. The plants will grow quickly in the full sun and moist soil.**

Plant your bog

A specialized group of plants thrives in a bog. Some of these unique plants are carnivorous while others are common easy-to-grow perennials. Check out these three bog-friendly perennials.

Add a bog to your pond

Hardworking bogs filter water and add valuable nutrients for plants and wildlife in ponds and streams. When designing your pond or stream, consider adding a bog. In addition to their water-cleaning functions, bogs add to the landscape by hosting a diverse array of water-loving plants, softening the edge of your aquascape.

PITCHER PLANT
A carnivorous plant that is surprisingly easy to grow, pitcher plant (*Sarracenia leucophylla*) adds flair to the bog garden. It requires acidic soil and at least six hours of sun a day. Zones 6–9.

SEDGE
Grasslike, sedge is beloved for its clump or low-arching mound of narrow leaves. Many cultivars are available. It grows well in sun or shade. Zones 5–10.

ROSE TURTLEHEAD
A fall bloomer, rose turtlehead has graceful 2-to 4-foot-tall stems topped with pink flowers. It has a tidy, upright habit and spreads slowly. Zones 3–8.

Bog garden building tips

Set the stage for a long-lasting, diverse bog garden with these building tips. Be sure to include a diverse collection of plants so you can revel in the unique colors, textures, and forms of bog plants.

MATERIALS LIST
Flexible liner
Bog garden plants
Mulch

1 REMOVE EXISTING PLANTS
Prevent weeds from the beginning by removing existing plants from the garden site. A nonselective herbicide, such as Round-Up, was used to kill the grass here. Remove the dead turf and excavate the bog.

2 MAKE WAY FOR DRAINAGE
Bog plants grow best in moist soil, not standing water. Using an awl, puncture the pond liner every foot or so around the edge of the feature to ensure that water does not pool in the bog garden.

3 ADD PLANTS
Design a bog garden as you would a traditional perennial garden. Plant tall plants near the center or back of the garden and situate low-growing plants near the edges. Top with a 2-inch-thick layer of mulch.

Put together a container water garden

Small pots like these are the right size for tabletop or patio water gardens. Move them as needed to serve as an instant centerpiece or focal point.

Kick off a water gardening adventure with a container water garden.

You can create one in an hour or two with no digging and little expense. And best of all, you can place your container water garden anywhere—from the center of your patio table to the center of a perennial garden.

Virtually any kind of container works for a water garden. If it holds water—or can be made to hold water—it can become a water garden. Here are some suggestions: oversize dishes and bowls, ceramic or terra-cotta planting containers, wooden buckets, livestock troughs (older ones that are no longer shiny; otherwise they can be toxic), and galvanized buckets. When you have a choice, select a container that has a dark interior to give the illusion of greater depth and discourage algae growth.

It's easy to waterproof a nonwatertight container. Line containers with an inexpensive piece of flexible liner. Attach the liner to the container with strong glue or caulk. Seal the drainage hole in pottery containers with a scrap of liner spread with caulk. Pottery containers can also be used as a cache pot that holds a watertight plastic tub, available at home improvement stores. The pretty pottery will disguise the lackluster black plastic tub.

Add movement

Fountains help oxygenate the garden and add interest to your oasis. The fountainhead, size of the pump, and volume of the container must complement each other for the container garden to work seameslessly. Avoid large, high sprays; choose a spray pattern in keeping with the container style. Small spitting fountains, those that produce a tiny spray of water, are well suited to containers.

A container garden fountain calls for a small pump. A 30 to 45 gph pump is ideal for most containers. Drape the pump's electric cord over the back of the container and hide it among plants or bury it under gravel. A solar pump is another option.

TEST GARDEN TIP

Seal the interior

Seal the inside of glazed, galvanized, and terra-cotta pots with three coats of a urethane spray. The urethane prevents terra-cotta and glazed pots from weeping. Use it on galvanized and iron containers to protect them from rust. Apply three coats to the inside of the pot.

Creative containers

When choosing a container for your water garden, take advantage of the opportunity to recycle a vintage vessel. Cast-off buckets, water troughs, mixing bowls, garden urns, and a multitude of other containers will make fine planting places for your favorite miniature water lilies and floating plants.

Hunt for these treasures at tag sales, flea markets, and salvage yards. You'll likely be able to bring home water-garden-worthy containers for just a few dollars.

If a container has a small hole or two, don't worry. Seal the interior using the easy techniques in the Test Garden Tip above.

Container water garden tips

Container water gardens, just like ponds and pools,
can host a variety of water plants. For a balanced ecosystem, aim to cover 50 to 60 percent of the water surface with plants.

Choose plants in keeping with the scale of your container. Petite fairy moss, miniature cattail, and iris are good choices for containers. Plants that trail over the edges, such as parrot's feather, with its feathery leaves and curling stems, also work well. Miniature water lilies and small lotus are good. Plants reminiscent of water lilies, such as water poppy (*Hydrocleys nymphoides*) or water snowflake (*Nymphoides indica*), thrive in containers.

Above: **Measuring about 3 feet wide, this large shallow pot has plenty of space for marginal plants, a miniature water lily, and even a small fountain.**

Container water garden building tips

Think of a container water garden as a miniature pond. A container that is at least 3 feet wide and 1 foot or more deep provides plenty of space for a fountain, fish, and plants.

MATERIALS LIST

Watertight container
Pea gravel
Bricks or pavers
Small fountain and pump
Water plants
Goldfish

1 GO SOLAR
Rest a solar-powered pump on a bed of pea gravel. This eliminates the need to place the container garden near an electrical outlet.

2 ELEVATE PLANTS
Small pavers or bricks make perfect risers for potted plants. Elevate plants so they are an inch or two below the water surface.

3 USE A TOPPER
Spread a ½-inch layer of pea gravel over the potted plants to prevent them from dislodging when you add water.

4 ADD WATER
Fill the garden with regular tap water. If you are adding fish, make the water fish-friendly by adding products to remove the chlorine and chloramine.

5 GO GOLD
Goldfish are excellent for container water gardens. They grow slowly and will readily adapt to container garden conditions. Bring the fish indoors for winter.

ASK THE GARDEN DOCTOR

The plants in my container garden have grown like crazy. What can I do?

ANSWER: It's time to prune and divide your water garden. Begin by carefully removing the floating plants. Tease apart the roots and replace those plants that you wish to save. Add extra plants to a larger pond (but not in any public waterway) or toss them in the compost pile. Next remove water lilies and other potted plants. Divide each plant in half, repot it, and return half of the original plant to the container garden.

Container water gardens are quickly overcome by vigorously growing water plants; don't hesitate to prune and divide them every few weeks.

caring for water gardens

With a little help from you, your water garden will sparkle with clear water and healthy plants and fish. Use the tips and list on the following pages as your guide.

p.**156**
A HEALTHY WATER GARDEN

Easy-care water gardens work with nature to create a healthy ecosystem. Find out how to build the partnership.

p.**158**
CLEANING

Leaves and muck collect in the bottom of water gardens. Scoop out the debris every few years for the best water quality.

p.**160**
SEASONAL CARE

Water garden care is easy with quick-read charts that outline essential water, plant, critter, and equipment care for every season.

p.**168**
GARDEN DOCTOR

Your water garden questions answered! Check out this important advice, such as how to prevent algae.

p.**172**
MANAGING PESTS

Pests invade the garden from time to time. Learn how to send them packing and keep your garden in top shape.

Create a balanced ecosystem

Smart water garden management

will set the scene for a low-maintenance, pretty backyard oasis. Use the following tips as a guide for creating and caring for your garden. From small container gardens to sprawling ponds, these pointers will put you on the path of working together with nature to care for your garden.

Use all the elements. Plants and other pond life work together. Fish are not required in the water garden, but they do consume mosquito larvae and add lively interest to the pond. Floating plants provide shade, and they cool and filter the water and help control algae.

Submerged plants are also filters, and they feed fish as well as create shelter and spawning areas for them. Plant one cluster of submerged plants for every 2 square feet of pond surface. Also stock the pond with snails, which feed on algae.

Know your water. Invest in a kit for testing pond water. Kits are inexpensive, and several types are available. Test for ammonia and nitrite levels when you first fill your pond and then periodically thereafter, particularly if fish look stressed. If the pond develops a chemical problem, a partial water change will help lower ammonia and nitrite levels.

Above: **A well-balanced pond ecosystem includes plants above and below the water surface. Submerged plants help filter harmful chemicals out of the water.**

Keep the pond filled. Don't let the water garden evaporate—a drop of an inch or more below the normal water level starts to create unhealthy concentrations of salts and minerals and exposes the liner to deteriorating UV rays.

When you add water, fill the pond with just a trickle from a hose (place it at the bottom of the water garden) to allow fish and other pond life to adapt to the gradual changes in temperature and pH. Add no more than 10 to 20 percent of the total volume at any one time or the fish could go into shock. If you are using municipal water, add chloramine remover to the pond whenever you top it off.

If a chemical problem develops, partially change the water. To freshen the pond, drain it by about 10 percent of its capacity, preferably by drawing water from the bottom, where concentrations of harmful substances are highest. Then refill it as described. It's best to do this right before a rain, so rainfall can replace at least some of the water.

Provide aeration. Whether from a fountain or waterfall, splashing water keeps the garden well oxygenated, which is essential for supporting fish. Oxygenated water also stays fresh, warding off foul-smelling bacteria that thrive in a low-oxygen environment.

Remove leaves and debris. Debris decomposes and fouls water if not removed.

Skim leaves, fallen petals, and other floating plant matter from the bottom and surface of the pond with a net or by hand.

Pinch off yellowing and dying leaves. In fall, put netting over the pond to catch falling leaves, or make skimming the pond a daily routine. In late fall, when you remove the pump for winter, make sure the water is free of debris before the pond ices over.

Keep it under control. If fish populations increase too quickly, give some fish away. Regularly thin aggressive plants and divide overgrown plants so no single element takes over. Aim to maintain a maximum of 60 percent foliage cover of a pond's surface.

Consider a filter. If the water garden has continuing problems with debris, too much light, or excessive fish waste, consider adding a biological filter to the pond setup.

Prevent runoff. When applying chemicals to the lawn and plants surrounding your water garden, avoid letting the materials run off or trickle into the water. They can be toxic to fish and may promote algae growth in the water.

Feed fish properly. Feeding too much or too often fouls the water and necessitates a larger filter. Feed fish only when they are ravenous, and give them only as much as they can eat in about 10 minutes. Stop feeding fish when the water temperature drops below 50°F.

TEST GARDEN TIP

Encourage tadpoles

Algae are a favorite food of tadpoles (young frogs or toads). Tadpoles often feed in large groups along the side of a pond. They often occur naturally in water gardens. If you don't have them, scoop up some in a jar from a local creek or pond. Once established in a pond, frogs or toads will return naturally year after year.

Left: **By devouring algae-causing elements, fish, such as these butterfly koi, help to maintain clear pond water.**

Cleaning

Every three or four years your water garden will probably benefit from a good mucking out and cleaning. Unlike an active gardener's garage or garden shed, which becomes a catchall for everything from rakes to plastic pots and needs an annual cleaning to prevent chaos, a well-maintained water garden requires only infrequent cleaning.

Cleaning a water garden properly requires an investment of time and effort. A medium to large container garden can be cleaned in an hour or two, but a pond or stream demands a day's worth of effort.

The best time to clean a water garden is late summer to early fall. If the garden has fish, do the work on a cool day, which is easier on the fish, at least a month before winter sets in to give the fish enough time to recover. In warm climates, wait until plants go dormant and the water temperature is around 60°F.

Go fishing
Begin cleaning by draining your water feature. You can bail the water, or if you have a submersible pump, replace the output piping

Above: **Decaying plant debris will quickly foul pond water. Before winter sets in be sure to scoop all dead leaves and stems out of the garden.**

with a hose. Run the hose out of the water feature and siphon the water. While you wait for the level to drop, clean the filters.

A partially empty pond makes it easier to catch fish. Net them when the water is drained to 6 inches and place them in a bucket of pond water. After catching a few, transfer them to a 30-gallon trash can or an untreated (for algae) child's wading pool in the shade. This holding pen should be filled the day before with half pond and half fresh water, treated to remove chlorine and chloramine. Cover the holding pen with netting so the fish don't jump out. Don't feed the fish. If they are going to be held for more than an hour, put an aerator in the container.

Continue to remove water from the pond until only several inches remains in the bottom. Then stop pumping and check the muck for small fish and frogs, tadpoles, and other animals. Put these in a bucket with pond water.

Haul out the plants

Next, remove the plants, taking care that their foliage remains wet or damp so they survive the out-of-water experience. Wrap the foliage and pots in wet newspaper and set the plants in the shade, or submerge them in a wading pool or in buckets of water.

Bail the remaining water and pour it onto flowerbeds and the rest of the landscape. Don't pour it down the drain; it will clog plumbing. Scoop mud from the pond bottom, taking care not to damage the liner. Add the mud to the compost pile.

Clean and refill

Once the water garden is empty, hose it down. Use a soft brush to clean the sides of the liner. There is no need to use soap or other cleaners. Scrubbing also removes beneficial bacteria and helpful algae, so don't scrub too thoroughly. After hosing down the pond, remove the dirty water. Make any necessary repairs, especially if you have detected a leak. Divide and repot rootbound plants.

Next, fill the pond about halfway and add the plants. Then continue filling the water garden, preparing the water in the same way as for the garden's first stocking, adding chlorine and chloramine removers if necessary. Return the frogs and scavengers to the pond.

Check the fish for diseases and treat them if necessary. Then gently place them in water-filled plastic bags. Float the bags on the surface until the water temperature inside the bags is close to the pond temperature.

Water smarts Municipalities often treat water with chlorine and chloramine. Both chemicals kill fish, but fortunately there are removal treatments that work almost instantly. You can find products at home improvement stores and garden centers. Follow label instructions.

If you are just topping off your pond and adding less than 10 percent of the volume of water already in the pond, there is no need to dechlorinate. However if you are adding more than 10 percent, add a dechlorination treatment to neutralize the chlorine.

Chloramine is more harmful to fish. You should add a chloramine treatment each time you top off the pond. If you add about 5 percent of the water volume, treat the pond with 5 percent of the quantity needed to treat the entire pond.

Spring care

As water slowly warms in spring, the plants and creatures that call your water garden home begin to wake up from their winter slumber. Set the scene for a long, healthy growing season with these tips for caring for all parts of the garden.

PLANTS

WEED AND MULCH. Pluck away weeds as soon as you see them in early spring. They are much easier to eradicate when they are small and easy to pull, plus getting rid of weeds now will eliminate the risk of the weeds producing seeds and multiplying rapidly as soon as summer hits. Add a 2- to 3-inch layer of dense, hardwood mulch to keep weeds at bay. Do not use "weed and feed" products near a water feature; they may harm fish.

REPOSITION PLANTS. Return aquatic plants kept indoors over winter to the garden. Or if you moved plants to the deepest part of the pond, relocate them to shelves or risers for the growing season. Wait until the water reaches about 40°F before moving plants.

ADD NEW PLANTS. Now is a great time to add new plants to the water garden. Marginal, submerged, and floating plants will quickly establish roots before the water and air temperatures rise in summer.

DIVIDE AND REPOT. As you relocate hardy aquatic plants from their overwintering location to their summer growing spot, keep an eye out for any overgrown or rootbound plants. Crowded, intertwined roots extending to the edge of a container is a sign that a plant needs division.

WATER

SKIM DEBRIS. Use a rake or pond skimmer to gather leaves and other debris that collected in the water garden during winter. Add the nutrient-rich debris to your compost pile.

LET ALGAE APPEAR. A burst of algae bloom as the water temperature rises is of little concern and will quickly subside as soon as the ecosystem achieves a natural balance. Spring algae bloom is a natural occurrence.

COLLECT RAINWATER. Free of chlorine and chloramine, which are commonly found in tap water, rainwater is perfect for quickly and safely adding to your feature.

FISH

CAUTIOUSLY BEGIN FEEDING. As water warms, fish will slowly resume activity. When the water temperature hits 50°F, begin feeding fish, minimally at first, with a high-carbohydrate food.

SPEND TIME WITH FISH. Watch fish closely for signs of sores, parasites, or lethargic behavior. Treat problems as soon as you notice them.

TEST WATER WEEKLY. As fish become more active, the water chemistry will change. Use a pond testing kit to check ammonia and nitrite levels weekly. If the levels are high, decrease feeding fish until the biofilter takes effect and the water returns to balance.

EQUIPMENT

RECONNECT PUMP AND FILTER. If you stored the pump and filter, take time to clean them thoroughly if you did not do so before storage, and add them to the pond. If the pump overwintered in the pond, pull it out and clean the filter. If your pump includes a UV clarifier, be sure to replace the bulb.

CLEAN WATER GARDEN LIGHTS. Using a soft cloth, wipe debris from lights so they will shine brightly. Replace burned-out bulbs.

START A BIOLOGICAL FILTER. A biological filter begins to function when the water temperature reaches 50°F. Prime the filter by adding beneficial nitrifying bacteria.

Right: **There is much to do when the garden springs to life after a long winter. Spend time now preparing the water garden for a successful season.**

Debris collects in the pond at the end of a stream like this one. Use a pond vacuum to remove the muck without emptying the pond.

TEST GARDEN TIP

Consider a pond vacuum

Pond vacuums make it possible to gather muck, leaves, and other debris from the bottom of a pond without draining away the water. Light-duty vacuums are well suited for small ponds that don't collect too much debris. Powered by a garden hose to generate suction, these vacuums are available for about $100 at garden centers and home improvement stores that stock pond supplies. Large ponds and those with several inches of debris, can be cleaned by a more powerful electrically powered pond vacuum.

Dividing water lilies

Encourage water lilies to produce a summer-long bloom show by dividing overgrown plants in spring. Easy to divide, water lilies establish new roots quickly, and the divisions will likely bloom several weeks after they are divided.

1 WASH AWAY SOIL
Carefully wash soil from the rhizomes to find the small "eyes" or growth points that have sprouted. A water lily rhizome will produce anywhere from 3 to more than 10 growth points.

2 LOOK FOR GROWTH
Look for growth points that have a few leaves and roots—these will make good divisions. Use a sharp knife to cut these growth points from the main root; be sure to keep the leaves and root intact on the division. Allow the leafless and rootless growth points to remain on the main root.

3 REPOT
Repot the new starts in fresh soil so that the growth points are just at the soil surface. Firm the soil in place, and add a 2-inch layer of pea gravel. Be careful not to cover the growth points.

Summer care

The water garden teems with activity in summer. Water lilies and water cannas unfurl new blooms. Butterflies and birds gather nourishment in and around your oasis, and fish, turtles, frogs, and other creatures raise their young. Use the following tips to create the best environment possible for these natural wonders.

PLANTS

FERTILIZE PLANTS. Give water lilies, lotuses, and other water garden plants a boost by fertilizing them with aquatic plant food. Follow the directions on the package.

PLANT TROPICAL WATER LILIES. When the water temperature stays above 70°F, it's time to plant tropical water lilies and other tropical water garden plants. Take time to remove dead foliage and weak stems before placing the plants in your water garden.

REIN IN VIGOROUS PLANTS. Rake off overexuberant floating plants, especially if they cover more than 60 percent of the water's surface or cover the crowns of marginal plants. While you're in cleanup mode, remove spent flowers and yellowing foliage, and toss them in the compost pile, so they won't pollute the water.

WATER

TOP OFF WITH CARE. Summer evaporation accounts for the loss of up to 1 inch of water per week. While it doesn't sound like much, losing 1 inch of water can have a significant impact on pond creatures, especially in small water gardens. Top off your water garden as needed to maintain a consistent water level. Rainwater is a great source of water for the pond. It doesn't require antichlorine and chloramine treatment as tap water does. Collect rainwater in clean buckets and barrels.

KEEP THE WATER MOVING. Fish, combined with warm water temperatures, decrease the amount of oxygen available in the water. Oxygen is essential for aquatic creatures. An aerator, fountain, or any type of device that circulates water, will introduce valuable oxygen into the water.

CONTROL ALGAE NATURALLY. Submerged and floating plants , such as anacharis, water hyacinth, and water lettuce, control algae by absorbing nutrients from the water so effectively that they starve algae to death.

FISH

FEED HIGH-PROTEIN FOOD. As the water temperature rises above 60°F, switch from high-carbohydrate fish food to high-protein food. Be sure to give fish only as much food as they can eat in 10 minutes or so to prevent water quality problems.

TEST WATER WEEKLY. Using a pond water test kit, check the levels of ammonia and nitrite and also take a pH reading. If the pH rises above 8.0 or falls below 6.8, follow directions carefully when adding a pond remedy designed to change pH.

BE VIGILANT ABOUT PREDATORS. Netting, electric fencing, decoy predators, and motion detectors connected to impact sprinklers help deter problems. A watchful dog is effective too.

EQUIPMENT

LOOK FOR CHANGES IN FLOW RATE. If a waterfall or fountain begins running slowly, there's a good possibility that the pump intake or filter is clogged. The tubing may be kinked or the water line blocked. Inspect the feature immediately to prevent long-term damage to the pump, filter, and other pond equipment.

ADOPT A CLEANING ROUTINE. Clean the pump intake weekly. Remove debris from the skimmer every day or so. Clean the filter and water garden light lenses as need for efficient operation.

Above: **Summer is the prime season for water lilies. Take time to enjoy these gems when they are in bloom.**

Before heading out on summer vacation, be sure to top off your pond to prevent the water level from falling too low while you're away.

ASK THE GARDEN DOCTOR

I'll be on vacation for about a week this summer. Any tips for keeping my pond in top shape while I'm away?

ANSWER: Before you hit the road, take a couple hours to give your pond a good cleaning. Clean the pond filter. Remove any floating debris and be sure to empty the skimmer. Use a long-handled pond skimmer to collect leaves and other debris.

Fish in a planted pond can manage without food for about 2 weeks. If your pond does not have plants or you will be gone longer than a couple weeks, recruit a neighbor to feed the fish. Package up individual daily rations for your fish to simplify feeding for your neighbor.

Algae control

A mat of stringy green algae instantly erodes the beauty of your outdoor respite. Keep algae growth in check during summer by following these strategies. Implement several for best control.

1 ADD A UV CLARIFIER
A properly sized UV clarifier turns green water clear within a day.

2 RAKE ALGAE
Use a rake or brush to remove filamentous algae from the pond. Toss the algae in the compost pile.

3 PLANTS
Rely on submerged and floating plants to absorb nutrients that support vigorous algae growth.

4 TRY BARLEY STRAW
Before algae appears, add barley straw to the water garden. Enclosed in easy-to-use plastic containers or net bags, barley straw produces peroxide as it decomposes. Peroxide inhibits algae growth and is safe for plants and fish.

Fall care

Autumn is a color-filled season in and around the water garden. **Count on the glassy water surface to reflect the brilliant orange, red, and yellow tones of surrounding foliage. Fish and flowering plants will continue to flourish until frost blankets the garden.**

PLANTS

REMOVE TROPICAL FLOATING PLANTS. Frost will quickly turn the foliage of tropical plants to brown mush. Use a long-handled skimmer or a rake to quickly remove the debris from the pond before it sinks to the bottom and is tough to eradicate.

MOVE TROPICAL WATER LILIES INDOORS. Don't take any chances with tropical water lilies and cold temperatures—move these sensitive plants to a warmer location when nighttime temperatures drop to about 35°F. Remove the plants from their pots and trim off most of the leaves and roots. Repot the rhizomes in smaller containers and store them in an aquarium tank or other container where they get plenty of light and where the temperature can be maintained at about 68°F.

TRANSFER HARDY WATER LILIES TO DEEP WATER. In water gardens with an area that is 3 feet or deeper, move hardy water lilies to this deep zone after the first frost. They will safely overwinter there. If you have a shallow pond, see the overwintering instructions on opposite page.

WATER

INSTALL NETTING OVER THE POND. Before leaf fall, install netting over the pond to prevent leaves from landing in the water and decaying. Falling leaves can be problematic even if a tree canopy doesn't overhang your water garden. The wind will blow leaves from nearby trees to the pond, and you can count on marginal plants dropping leaves into the pond too.

IF NECESSARY, CLEAN THE POND. Fall is the best time for cleaning a pond. Most well-kept ponds require cleaning only every three or four years. Mild fall temperatures and end-of-season robust health make it easier for fish to withstand the stress associated with adjusting to new water conditions. For pond cleaning tips, see pages 158 to 159.

FISH

REDUCE FEEDING. Gradually stop feeding. When the water temperature drops below 60°F, switch from high-protein fish food that you used in summer to high-carbohydrate food. Cut back on feeding to every third day; gradually stop feeding fish when they show no appetite.

PROTECT FISH WITH A NET. Fish become inactive in late fall and through winter, resting on the pond bottom. Protect them from predatory birds by spreading a net over the surface of the pond.

EQUIPMENT

CHECK PUMPS AND FILTERS REGULARLY. Leaves clogging pumps and filters will quickly stress the equipment. Clean pump intakes and filters frequently in fall.

REMOVE FILTERS AND PUMPS. When the water temperature drops below 40°F, remove, clean, and store your mechanical filters and pump, as well as the biofilter and pump. Also remove the UV clarifier. Prior to storing the pumps and filters for winter, clean and dry them, with the exception of the biofilter—keep it wet or moist over winter to retain the good bacteria for next year.

Right: **Enjoy colorful fall foliage, but be vigilant about removing leaves before they pollute the pond water.**

TEST GARDEN TIP

Play ball!

At the end of summer, hit the pool toys clearance aisle and pick up a few beach balls. Blow up the balls and float them in your pond before covering it with netting. The balls will act as support under the netting, creating a tentlike environment that prevents fallen leaves from coming in contact with the water.

Left: **Stay on top of removing fallen leaves from the water feature to reduce harmful sediment buildup.**

Prepare hardy water lilies for winter

Hardy water lilies are simple to overwinter in a pond that is 3 feet or deeper—simply move them to the deep zone for winter. It requires a bit more effort to overwinter them in shallow ponds. Here are a couple methods; choose the one that is easiest for you.

1 PLASTIC BAG STORAGE

After the first frost, remove the containers of water lilies from the pond. Trim off all dead leaves and stems. Place the containers in plastic bags to maintain moisture. Store the water lilies in a cool basement or other area where the temperature will remain between 32 and 50°F. Check the plants regularly to make sure that there is plenty of moisture in the bags.

2 SPHAGNUM MOSS STORAGE

Hardy water lilies can also be overwintered in sphagnum moss. After the first frost, remove plants from the pond. Lift the rhizomes from the pots, pruning off all old leaves and stems. Store the rhizomes in damp sphagnum moss placed in plastic bags. Store the bags in a basement or other area where the temperature is 40 to 50°F.

Winter care

Depending on where you live, winter in the water garden might be a time of rest and relaxation for both you and your aquatic environment. If you live in a mild climate though, you'll enjoy the rush of a waterfall and the darting of fish in winter too. Take cues from nature when caring for your water garden this season.

PLANTS

CHECK HARDY WATER LILY PLANTS. If you are overwintering hardy water lilies outside the pond, check on them at least once a month. Be sure the soil or moss around the rhizomes is moist.

LEAVE PLANTS FOR COVER. Grasses and perennials at the edge of the water feature add interest to the garden in winter and may also offer protection for birds and wildlife.

ORDER NEW PLANTS. Prepare for spring by ordering new water garden plants for spring arrival. Some favorite water lilies and lotuses sell out quickly in spring, so place your order now to ensure you get to grow the plants on your wish list next season.

MILD CLIMATES: ADD COOL-SEASON COLOR. Light up the area around your water garden with cool-season flowering plants such as pansies and cyclamen. Add fun foliage interest with ornamental cabbage and kale.

WATER

MILD CLIMATES: FOLLOW SUMMER CARE TIPS. If you live in a mild-winter climate, other than raking out leaves that might collect in the water garden, your fall and winter care will not differ from summer care. Enjoy your garden year-round!

COLD CLIMATES: TAKE A BREAK. A frozen water feature is a carefree water feature. Kick back and dream about next year's garden during the chilly season.

FISH

DISCONTINUE FEEDING. If you haven't done so already, stop feeding fish especially once the water temperature dips below 45°F. Resist the urge to feed them during any midwinter warm spells. Cold temperatures quickly return, making the fish too cold to digest food. Undigested food spoils in a fish's gut, a sometimes fatal situation.

ADD A DEICER. Maintain a small amount of open water, allowing oxygen to reach the water and toxic gases to escape, by using a deicer. An electric deicer is a heating element attached to a float. It is connected to a 120-volt outlet with a GFCI. The deicer's thermostat turns on the heating element as the water temperature approaches freezing and turns it off as the surface water temperature rises above freezing, heating a small volume of water in its vicinity.

EQUIPMENT

REMOVE LEAF NETTING. Don't let a heavy snow load damage your leaf netting. Remove it from the pond in early winter and store it in a dry place until next fall.

DRAIN ABOVEGROUND PONDS. Aboveground pond liners are especially susceptible to cracking and breaking during the freeze-thaw cycles in winter. Eliminate the headache of repairing the liner by draining the feature in early winter.

WINTERTIME WATERFALL. Gardeners in mild climates enjoy their waterfalls year-round, but those in cold climates run the risk of damaged pipes and pumps from the freezing temperatures. If you live in a cold climate, shut down your waterfall, drain the pipes, and disconnect the pump.

Right: **When water features are at rest in winter, beckon a variety of songbirds with a nutritious seed mix.**

TEST
GARDEN
TIP

Minimize moving water

Discontinue using a pump if you install a deicer during winter. Using a pump when operating a deicer moves the warmed water away from the deicer, making it consume extra amounts of power to warm colder water. The constant fluctuation in water temperature will also disturb fish.

Cleaning and storing a pump
In cold climates, as you prepare the garden for winter, remember to care for your pond equipment. Early winter is a great time to give your pump, filter, and other pond devices a good cleaning before placing them in storage. They will be ready to add to the pond as soon as spring arrives. (While gardeners in warm climates will not store their equipment during winter, this is still a great time to give it a good cleaning.) Follow these three easy steps for cleaning and storing your pump.

1 REMOVE
Remove the pump from the pond. Begin by disconnecting the pump from the electrical source. Carefully remove the pump from the pond.

2 CLEAN
For specific instructions for cleaning your pump, refer to the owner's manual. In general, use a soft bristle brush to clean the water intake and output areas, loosening debris that may be clogging the intake. Rinse with warm, clean water.

If the pump has a filter, remove and clean it using a strong stream of water. Dislodge debris and rinse well. Replace the filters after cleaning. If the pump includes a UV clarifier, replace the bulb.

3 STORE
Store your pump in a cool, dry location. Some manufacturers recommend storing pumps in a tub of water to prevent seals from drying out. Refer to the owner's manual for storage instructions.

Water feature problems and solutions

Occasional battles with algae, pond leaks, and plants that fail to perform are part of the challenge of tending a dynamic water garden. Here's a rundown of common problems and tips for prevention as well as timesaving solutions when problems do arise.

My pond is full of muck. How did this happen and what can I do about it?

ANSWER: Fallen leaves are most likely the source of your problem. In autumn, leaves fall on the water surface and after a few hours sink to the bottom of the pond or stream. In time the leaves decompose, forming the brown, sticky muck you encountered.

The best line of defense against leaves and other debris piling up on the bottom of your pond is to cover the feature with netting in fall. Be sure to anchor the netting on the sides with bricks or stakes driven into the soil. The netting will catch the leaves, and you can transport them to the compost pile before they decompose. Plan to empty the netting every few days.

As for the muck at the bottom of your pond, it's time to get wet and dirty! Scoop out the muck and leaves with your hand or a lightweight plastic rake. For larger ponds, especially those without many plants or fish, consider investing in a pond sweep or pond vacuum, which attaches to a garden hose and uses water pressure to remove debris and silt from the pond bottom.

There is a hole in my pond's flexible liner. How do I fix it?

ANSWER: Good news—once you identify the source of a leak, the repair process only takes a few minutes and requires basic supplies.

Begin by purchasing a flexible liner repair kit. Available at garden centers that stock water garden supplies and some home improvement stores, flexible pond liner repair kits make sealing a leak a cinch. The repair kit will include a piece of EPDM liner along with two-sided liner sealing tape. The kit might also include a roller to ensure a good seal.

Get started by drying the area around the leak. The patch material will adhere best to dry liner. Use a small piece of sandpaper to rough up the liner around the leak. The tape or glue securing the patch will easily adhere to this rough surface. Finally apply the patch as directed on the leak repair kit. Be sure to hold it securely in place as recommended to ensure a good seal.

There are 10 or 15 water testing kits at my local garden center. Do I need to buy multiple kits? What should I look for when making a purchase?

ANSWER: Several shelves of water testing kits can be overwhelming, but there is good news—you will likely need only one kit. Look for a kit that provides all of the following measurements.

pH Testing the water's pH will help you determine if your water is within the desired range of 6.5 to 7.5 for healthy plants and fish. Keep in mind many fish will tolerate some deviation from this range. Extremely acid water can be countered through the addition of pure household baking soda. Begin by adding 1 teaspoon per 500 gallons of water. Treat extremely alkaline water with household white vinegar. Begin by adding ¼ cup per 500 gallons of water.

Chlorine Although chlorine will dissipate in a few hours or days, it can be harmful to aquatic plants and fish. A test kit will help you gauge the amount of chlorine and chloramine in your pond water, giving you confidence to add dechlorinator or chloramine treatment when necessary.

Nitrite and nitrate If your water garden includes fish, be sure your test kit screens for nitrite and nitrate levels. Nitrite is toxic at any level and can be persistent in a new pond. Nitrate, by comparison, is relatively harmless unless it rises above 50 ppm. A test kit will tell you when you need to take action.

I need to add water to my pond. Can I simply run water into it from my garden hose? Do I need to treat the water first?

ANSWER: City tap water often contains chlorine, chloramine, and various chemicals. Check with your local utility to learn what chemicals are used to treat public water. If you are just topping off your pond (adding up to 10 percent of the total volume), the chlorine will dissipate in a few hours and not cause problems.

Chloramine, on the other hand, is a powerful antimicrobial agent that is harmful to plants and fish. Chloramine must be removed. Add a chloramine treatment (which also removes chlorine) each time you top off the pond. If you add about 5 percent of the water volume, treat the pond with 5 percent of the quantity needed to treat the entire pond. If you are filling your pond for the first time, plan to wait two to three weeks after filling it to add fish. The water will begin to establish an equilibrium. The chlorine and chloramine levels will not be a threat, and the pH will likely be in the optimum range.

Water feature problems and solutions

My water feature is constantly losing water. How do I figure out what is going on?

ANSWER: There are several potential reasons why your pond is losing water. Here are some of the most common causes and the best solutions.

Consider evaporation. High temperatures and wind will quickly evaporate pond water. Evaporation is especially noticeable in small water features. A 1- to 2-inch drop in the water level a week during the warmest period of summer is common. If the water level drops more than 1 to 2 inches, look into other causes of the problem.

Is wind a factor? Wind accounts for some water loss around fountains and waterfalls. Even a small amount of wind will increase evaporation and send a fountain spray outside the retention basin. Prevent wind-induced water loss by partially surrounding the feature with dense shrubs or a decorative fence.

Look for a liner leak. A small tear in the liner will result in greater water loss than you might imagine. Water will slowly seep out of the pond 24 hours a day, and the water level will drop quickly. Find the tear by allowing the water to leak from the pond—be sure to remove fish or plants if the water level drops too low. When the water stops leaking, carefully inspect the liner at the water level. The rip or tear is likely very near the water level or slightly above or below.

Repair the leak using a pond liner patch kit available at your local garden center. Apply the patch and allow it to dry for at least 24 hours.

A few months ago I purchased a new submersible pump. It recently stopped working. Is this normal? What is the lifespan of a submersible pump?

ANSWER: With proper care, a good-quality water garden pump should last for several years. For longest life, make sure debris and algae don't tax the motor. Clean the intake filter at least once a week during spring and up to three times a week in summer and fall.

Make sure the pump isn't sitting directly on the pond bottom, where it will take in more silt. Set it on a brick or flat stone. If algae clog the pump, clean the pump and make an additional filter by wrapping the pump in a large piece of fiberglass window screen; then place it inside a black plastic basket. Never run the pump without water. It will burn out the motor.

I added water lilies to my garden this year. It's near the end of the season, and the plants have produced only a couple blooms. What can I do to encourage them to bloom more?

ANSWER: Water lilies are jewels of the water garden, and they thrive when their needs are met. Check out this list of growing tips and modify the conditions in and around your pond if possible to encourage more blossoms.

Sun is essential. Most, but not all, water lilies require eight hours or more of sunlight a day. Trees and shrubs near the water's edge may cast shadows, preventing water lilies from getting adequate sunlight. Tall marginal plants such as cattails and water cannas can block light too.

Calm water is preferred. Splashing from a fountain or waterfall disturbs water lilies and prevents them from growing and blooming vigorously. If your plants are affected by moving water, relocate them to another part of the garden where they can grow in a peaceful environment.

Check the planting depth. Water lilies grow near the soil surface. Their rhizomes are best planted so the growing point, or eye, is level with the soil surface. Water lilies that are planted too deep will grow slowly and bloom sporadically, if at all.

Look for rootbound plants. Water lilies grow best in broad, shallow containers in which they can spread freely. Plants that have grown to the edge of the container will be stressed. Leaf size will diminish and flowering will slow down or halt entirely. Plants pushing out the sides of their containers indicate that it is time to divide and repot. Another sign that the plants need to be repotted is when the buds rot off before they make it to the surface. This indicates the plant is running out of nutrients.

My filter isn't working well. How do I clean it?

ANSWER: Filters work to strain debris from pond water. In that process, they collect all sorts of debris in the foam, rocks, plastic balls, or other media that make up the filter. It's essential to rinse the particles out of the filter layers so the filter can function at maximum capacity.

The method you use to clean the filter depends on the type of filter it is. To clean the pads of a mechanical filter, lift the filter layer out of the filter unit and spray it with a burst of water from a hose for a minute or two. Replace the filter pads annually.

The best way to clean a biofilter is to gently rinse the filter pads with pond water. Your goal is to dislodge debris and harmful bacteria while maintaining the beneficial bacteria and enzymes that make the filter function. Most biological filters benefit from an annual cleaning in winter when pond bacteria and organisms are less active. It takes as long as eight weeks for the beneficial bacteria in the filter to reestablish, making winter the ideal time to thoroughly clean your filter. See the filter user's guide for instructions.

All filters function best with frequent cleaning. Plan to rinse your filter pads as often as once a day in summer when plants and fish are most active. In other seasons pads may require cleaning only once a week. Use water quality and amount of particles collected as a guide for how often to rinse your filter.

Water garden pest patrol

Water gardens, just like other areas of the landscape,

are susceptible to pest attacks from time to time. The prevalence of pests in your garden is influenced by your location—suburban landscapes are often challenged by different pests than those on acreages or in dense urban environments. Climate also has a great impact. Prevalent pests in the desert Southwest, for example, are different from those that attack gardens in the Northeast.

The plants and animals that call your garden home also influence the pest population. You can count on some plants to attract beneficial insects, which devour aphids and other pests. A pond stocked with fish attracts raccoons, herons, and other meat eaters. Remember, garden pests are as unique as the garden they inhabit. Pests attacking your garden are not necessarily the same pests munching in your neighbor's patch down the road.

Above: **The plants growing in and around a water garden influence the pests that are attracted to the area. Fortunately, most aquatic plants are relatively pest-free.**

Opposite top: **Take time to positively identify potential pests so you can effectively control them.**

Insects and diseases

Water garden plants are generally fuss-free, only occasionally falling prey to insects or diseases. Leaf miners, aphids, and Japanese beetles munch or burrow inside leaves, reducing the plant's ability to make food and maintain strong defense against further attacks.

If you think a plant has a pest problem, watch to see what changes take place over the following days or weeks. Does the entire plant or just a portion of the plant show signs of decline? Has another type of insect arrived on the scene, perhaps to consume the first? Is the damage simply cosmetic and not harming the plant?

Depending on the type of insect, the damage, the weather conditions, and your goals for the plant, you may not need to intervene at all.

Animal pests

Raccoons, birds, deer, snapping turtles, and many other animals can thwart your efforts to create a beautiful, low-maintenance water garden. Carnivores, such as raccoons and herons, use a pond stocked with fish as a tasty food source. Deer and snapping turtles are known to devour succulent water lily buds and leaves.

Fence, netting, and scare devices are all effective against these smart creatures. Often you'll need to employ several lines of defense to limit unwanted fishing and feasting in your garden.

Invasive pond plants

Invasive plants in a perennial border cause headaches, but they can be a serious threat in a water garden. Aggressive pond plants, unlike their terrestrial counterparts, often prove to be more invasive and difficult to control if they escape into a natural habitat. They will quickly outcompete native species. Take these steps to prevent overly vigorous aquatic plants from spreading to natural areas.

Tried and true. Grow beloved and well-behaved water plants like water lilies and lotuses. No need to worry about these bearers of gorgeous blooms becoming invasive.

Beware of invasives. Australian swamp stonecrop (*Crassula helmsii*), mosquito fern (*Azolla pinnata*), and frogbit (*Hydrocharis morsus-ranae*) are particularly invasive and should be grown only in small container gardens. Or play it safe and do not grow them at all.

Search out natives. Ask your plant supplier or local extension service for aquatic plants native to your area.

Shop with care. Purchase plants from reputable suppliers that properly label their plants so you know what plant you are buying.

Compost extra plants. Do not transport extra plants to a nearby pond or body of water. Instead compost the extra plants to prevent the spread of invasive species.

Watch for "vigorous" or "fast growing." These terms on plant labels often indicate that the plants are potentially invasive if they find their way into the wild.

Pest remedies

Various creatures will visit or stay in your water garden throughout the gardening season. Most you won't notice, but some you'll quickly spot because of their size or the damage they cause. Focus on these common pests and what it takes to control them.

Raccoons
Water gardens offer a buffet for raccoons. They knock over plants and tear them apart in search of snails and insects in the soil. They also enjoy hunting frogs and catching fish that happen to swim by. Raccoons usually visit the water garden at dusk or in the early morning.

DAMAGE
Knocked over and dismantled pond plants are signs of raccoon feeding. Disturbed rocks and stones also indicate raccoons may have been in the area. If fish are disappearing, raccoons could be the culprits.

CONTROL
One way to deter raccoons is to design the pond so they don't have easy access to the fish in the first place. Raccoons like to wade in shallow water and are reluctant to venture into water that's more than 6 to 8 inches deep. If raccoons are common in your area, build a water feature more than a foot deep, without shallow shelves around the edges. Place marginal plants away from the edges and support them at the correct depth on bricks. These measures are also effective against opossums, which have habits similar to raccoons. A net covering the pond or a motion-sensitive sprinkler attached to your garden hose may also be a deterrent.

Bird pests
Herons and egrets stop by water gardens to feast on fish. Unlike raccoons, they are not dissuaded by straight pond sides or deep water. Kingfishers also dine in water gardens. You may hear their loud, rattling calls before they arrive.

DAMAGE
Missing fish accompanied by little or no damage to surrounding pond plants is an indication of bird pests. If plants have been disturbed as well, raccoons are more likely the problem.

CONTROL
Herons are territorial and less likely to visit a pond that appears to be inhabited by another heron. Artificial but real-looking herons are sold. Place the decoy heron on a post near the water garden. Deter kingfishers and egrets with 1- or 2-inch mesh netting stretched and supported across your pond. Do not use finer mesh; birds may become entangled.

Domestic cats
Your favorite feline might see your pond as a prime fishing spot. Cats many spend a lot of time gazing into the sparkling water, but they don't often go so far as catching their daily meal pondside. While they do get lucky once in a while, household felines are strictly dabblers when it come to fishing. One paw is as far as they'll go if water is involved.

DAMAGE
Cats swipe at and occasionally catch small fish. Goldfish, golden ofre, and young koi are all susceptible to feline fishing. Some dogs will swipe at and occasionally catch fish too.

CONTROL
If you see mischief during daylight hours, a gentle spray in the cat's direction with a garden hose will make him scamper away. Prevent nighttime fishing by keeping your cat indoors after dark.

Leaf miners
The larvae of small flies, leaf miners feed between the upper and lower surfaces of a leaf. Various leaf miner species infest different perennials at certain points in the growing season. The glossy green leaves of water lilies attract hungry leaf miners.

DAMAGE

Leaf miner feeding creates light green or yellow tunnel-like patterns on leaf surfaces. Damage is easy to spot on water lily pads.

CONTROL

Removing infested leaves or cutting plants to soil level and destroying clippings typically eliminates the problem. Leaf miners tend to gravitate to weedy areas; keep the garden cleaned up to help eradicate these pests.

Japanese beetle
The adult Japanese beetle feeds on flowers and leaves of various perennials, such as thalia, water canna, and daylily. When the beetles find a food source, they release a scent that attracts more beetles. Females lay eggs in the ground, which hatch into grubs, a major lawn pest.

DAMAGE

Adult beetles eat leaf tissue between the veins, creating a skeletonized effect. The may also eat large holes in flower petals.

CONTROL

Control grubs in your lawn and you'll reduce the number of Japanese beetles (unless your neighbor doesn't control grubs, in which case beetles will invade your garden). A fungus called milky spore controls grubs but may take a few years to build up an effective concentration. Knock beetles from plants into a container of soapy water. Adult beetle traps are ineffective and may lure more beetles than you already have in your garden.

Aphids
Soft-bodied insects that suck plant sap, aphids cluster along tips of new growth. Look for white or greenish shed skins along with the insects. Aphids can spread plant viruses, which makes them doubly problematic. Most active in cool weather, aphids tend to disappear as summer heat builds and predators and parasites that destroy aphids multiply.

DAMAGE

New growth may be distorted. Aphids secrete sugary honeydew, a sticky, shiny substance that may speckle leaves. Black sooty mold grows in honeydew and remains until rain washes it off. In severe infestations, ants will scurry along infested plant stems, feeding on the honeydew.

CONTROL

Use a jet of water from the hose to dislodge aphids or insecticidal soap to kill them. Avoid overfertilizing and overwatering, which promote the lush growth that aphids favor. Ladybugs, syrphid flies, and aphidiid wasps control aphids, but you must allow aphids to increase to 10 to 20 per shoot tip for beneficial insects to lay eggs and counteract the pest.

plant encyclopedia

Learn about the hundreds of plants that will thrive in and around your water garden. Pretty and hardworking, water garden plants support wildlife, improve water quality, and decorate your garden with exquisite blossoms.

SUBMERGED PLANTS

Industrious, but rarely seen, submerged plants are pros at filtering harmful substances out of the water.

FLOATING PLANTS

Painting the water surface with color, these plants thrive in all water gardens. Choose some for your garden.

MARGINAL PLANTS

Shallow water or moist soil is just right for moisture-loving marginal plants. Add some to the edges of your pond or stream.

RAIN GARDEN PLANTS

A host of perennials and shrubs that thrive in both wet and dry soil, rain garden plants offer good-looking foliage and flowers all season.

Anacharis
(*Egeria densa*)

Anacharis has shiny, bright green leaves that resemble fluffy feather dusters. It's a pro at oxygenating pond water. It is vigorous, so grow it with care.

Where to plant
Anacharis grows underwater in sun or shade. An adaptable plant, it grows well in water ranging from 1 to 10 feet deep and will spread to 10 feet. It also grows well in a container. Anacharis is hardy in Zones 8 to 11.

Growing
Plant anacharis in a large, shallow container filled with sand or small gravel. The plant's creeping runners will expand slowly to form a colony. If you are growing anacharis in a container garden, simply plant it in sand or small gravel spread on the bottom of the pot. Look for its three-petal white flowers floating on the water surface in summer.

Special notes
To overwinter anacharis in cold climates, bring in stem cuttings and keep them in an aquarium, where they will quickly root and grow.

Arrowhead
(*Sagittaria* spp.)

Arrowhead earns its name from its distinctive leaf shape. Its strong vertical presence makes it a great plant for adding height among low-growing water plants.

Where to plant
Arrowhead grows best in full sun or part shade and moist soil or submerged about 2 inches below the water surface. It grows 3 to 24 inches tall and spreads by vigorous underground stems. It is hardy in Zones 3 to 11.

Growing
Plant arrowhead in a wide, shallow container filled with heavy garden soil. Arrowhead has single white flowers held on long stalks that rise from the center of the plant. They appear first in June and continue through summer. Hardy varieties of arrowhead will overwinter in the pond. Move tender varieties to a moist, cool, dark location during winter.

Special notes
Common arrowhead (*S. sagittifolia*) grows to 18 inches. Ruby-eye arrowhead, or giant arrowhead, (*S. montevidensis*) has red dots at the base of each petal. It is 2 feet tall and hardy to Zone 8. Lanceleaf arrowhead (*S. lancifolia*) has yellow-centered blooms and grows to 2 feet. It is hardy to Zone 8.

Big bluestem
(*Andropogon gerardii*)

Blue-green foliage, purple flower plumes, and brilliant bronze fall color make big bluestem a showy member of the rain garden. It offers color and texture year-round.

Where to plant

This native grass grows best in full sun and average garden soil. Big bluestem has a big presence in the garden. It grows 4 to 7 feet tall and will reach 10 feet tall in optimal growing conditions. It spreads to form a clump that is 3 to 4 feet wide. The plant is hardy in Zones 4 to 9.

Growing

Big bluestem grows best in moderately drained soil; plant it on the outskirts of a rain garden, where it is less likely to be submerged in water. It tolerates drought well. In spring, cut big bluestem back to about 6 inches above the soil. It will send up new shoots as soon as soil and air temperatures rise.

Special notes

'Silver Sunrise' is a 5- to 6-foot-tall variety with blue-green foliage that is striped with a yellow band. The foliage turns purple in fall. 'Pawnee' is a popular variety that also grows 5 to 6 feet tall. Its blue-green foliage turns light red in fall.

Black-eyed susan
(*Rudbeckia hirta*)

This sturdy perennial infuses the garden with long-lasting color, flowering from early summer to fall. If the plant grows too vigorously, simply pull out unwanted stems.

Where to plant

Plant black-eyed susan in full sun. It will tolerate part shade but will not bloom as prolifically. It grows well in all types of soil—from sandy to clay—and thrives in soil that has average fertility. Plants grow 24 to 30 inches tall and 24 to 36 inches wide. Black-eyed susan is hardy in Zones 3 to 10.

Growing

After planting, water the transplants regularly until they are established. After that, drought tolerance reigns and plants require little water or fertilizer. Deadheading regularly promotes rebloom and prevents excessive reseeding.

Special notes

'Indian Summer' grows 3 to 4 feet tall and 1 foot wide. It has golden yellow petals surrounding black centers. 'Prairie Sun' is 30 inches tall and 12 to 18 inches wide. It is a yellow daisy with a green center. 'Toto' is a small plant growing just 10 inches tall and 12 inches wide. Its 4-inch flowers are golden with a brown center.

YOU SHOULD KNOW
Black-eyed susan is relatively pest-free, although during the wet conditions that exist from time to time in rain gardens it can develop fungal leaf spot disease. Thin the planting to promote good air circulation and reduce disease incidence.

Cattail
(*Typha* spp.)

A North American native and a favorite nesting plant for birds, cattail adds a striking vertical element to the garden. Grow it in moist soil or standing water.

Where to plant

Cattail grows best in full sun or part shade and moist soil or submerged up to 4 inches below the water surface. There are giant and dwarf forms of cattail. Plant height can range from 6 inches to more than 12 feet. It is hardy in Zones 3 to 11.

Growing

Plant cattail in a wide, shallow container filled with heavy garden soil. Plants overwinter well in standing water and withstand freezing temperatures. In early spring, cut stems and foliage back to about 6 inches above the soil level. The plant will send up new stems.

Special notes

Common cattail (*T. latifolia*) is the standard cattail seen in ditches and wetlands. It is excellent for water filtration. Graceful cattail (*T. laxmannii*) is narrow leafed with foliage that arches and sways. This very elegant plant is suitable for most ponds and large container water gardens. Dwarf cattail (*T. minima*) grows just 18 inches tall and has pretty blue-green foliage and miniature catkins.

Common duckweed
(*Lemna minor*)

Known as the smallest flowering plant in the world, duckweed is food for fish in spring and fall thanks to its excellent tolerance of cool temperatures.

Where to plant

Duckweed grows well in full sun or part shade. Grow it in water gardens of all sizes—from tiny container gardens to large ponds. It has round or almost-round light green leaves less than ⅛ inch in diameter, with a single root growing from under the leaf. Common duckweed is hardy in Zones 3 to 11.

Growing

Plant common duckweed in spring just after ice leaves the pond. Its pleasing, delicate texture will complement all types of companion plants. If duckweed gets out of control, use a rake to pull it off the surface or drag a 2×4 plank across the water surface to skim off excess.

Special notes

It is essential to have goldfish or koi in a water garden with common duckweed. When planted in a garden without fish, common duckweed will quickly overtake the pond in a single season.

YOU SHOULD KNOW If your pond does not contain fish, fill it with tap water. Municipal water usually contains chloramines and chlorine in small quantities that don't harm plants (but they will harm fish). Go ahead and top off your pond with tap water anytime it needs a refill.

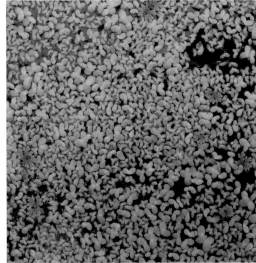

Eel grass
(*Vallisneria spiralis*)

Moving gracefully like an eel in a slight current, eel grass is a great plant for growing at the base of a waterfall or in a deep stream. Fish like to hide in eel grass.

Where to plant

Eel grass grows underwater in sun or shade and tolerates moving water with ease. Grow it near a waterfall or the area where a stream spills into a pond. It produces 2- to 3-foot-long tapelike green leaves. Eel grass is hardy in Zones 4 to 11.

Growing

Plant eel grass in a large shallow container filled with sand or small gravel. The creeping runners will expand slowly to form a colony of swaying grass. Divide this lush grass anytime to expand your colony or share with friends.

Special notes

Eel grass is available in a variety of colors and shapes, with both red-leaf and twisted or curled foliage. 'Crystal' eel grass has a green, glassy look. 'Red Jungle' eel grass has broad burgundy foliage. Eel grass has dense upright foliage that is an ideal hiding place for fish as they take cover from predatory birds.

Elephant's ear
(*Alocasia* spp.)

A tropical plant, elephant's ear is a marginal plant prized for its bold, triangular leaves. The leaves can be green, yellow, bronze, blue-green, and variegated and up to 3 feet long.

Where to plant

Elephant's ear, also called alocasia, thrives in part or full shade and warm, humid conditions. It grows well in moist or waterlogged soil. It is hardy in Zones 10–11

Growing

Plant elephant's ear in a large container filled with garden soil placed in water so that the edge of the pot is a couple of inches below the water surface. Elephant's ear will also grow along the edge of a pond or stream.

It is a heavy feeder so fertilize plants every two weeks. Overwinter it by digging up the tuber in fall and storing it in a cool, dry place until spring. Stored tubers carried over for several years produce massive plants.

Special notes

'Grandis' elephant's ear (*A. loweii* 'Grandis') has dark green leaves with scalloped edges and bold white veins. 'Grandis' leaves are purple on the underside. 'Lutea' elephant's ear (*A. macrorrhiza* 'Lutea') has thick yellow leaf stems and veins.

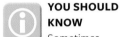 **YOU SHOULD KNOW** Sometimes gardeners are led to believe that their water garden will reach a "natural equilibrium"—a state at which everything is in balance so the pond rarely needs cleaning or fertilizing— if they follow a mathematical formula of plants and fish.

Unfortunately, this is not true. Water gardens are dynamic artificial environments. All parts of the garden contribute to overall health and well-being. Since gardens change daily, ratios and rules are helpful guides but they don't eliminate all the work. Experience and experimentation will serve you well as you care for your garden.

Fanwort
(*Cabomba caroliniana*)
In summer, fanwort is decorated with tiny white flowers with a bright yellow center. The blossoms of this submerged plant often rise so they are at or near the water surface.

Where to plant
Easy-to-grow fanwort thrives in sun or shade and water that is 1 to 10 feet deep. Clusters of fanwort will expand to about 1 foot wide, and the stems will grow about 6 feet long. The plant is hardy in Zones 5 to 11.

Growing
Plant fanwort in a shallow container filled with sand or gravel. Tuck several leaves and stems under an inch or two of sand or gravel to anchor the plant. If fanwort becomes overly aggressive in your water feature, don't hesitate to remove entire clumps. It will reestablish if a few plants are left in place.

Special notes
Fanwort is aggressive and prohibited in several areas. Be sure to check with your state department of natural resources before planting. Where it can be grown, use it in container gardens to lessen the chances it will escape and establish in a native habitat. Fanwort's fluffy structure is excellent for goldfish spawning.

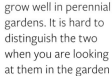

YOU SHOULD KNOW Some types of forget-me-nots grow well in ponds. Others grow well in perennial gardens. It is hard to distinguish the two when you are looking at them in the garden center. If a plant withers and dies in a pond setting, it belongs in a perennial garden.

Flowering rush
(*Butomus umbellatus*)
Add sparkle to the spring and early summer water garden with the airy pink or white, 4- to 5-inch-wide flowers of flowering rush. It's an easy-to-grow hardy perennial.

Where to plant
Flowering rush grows best in full sun or part shade. Plant it in moist soil at the water garden edge or submerged in up to 3 inches of water. It grows 3 to 4 feet tall and spreads 1 to 2 feet. The plant is hardy in Zones 3 to 7.

Growing
Plant flowering rush in a shallow pot filled with heavy garden soil. Because flowering rush is a rampant grower and can become invasive, it should always be planted in a pot, even when grown in a bog garden.

Once the heat of summer hits, flowering rush quits blooming or sometimes dies back altogether, but in cooler climates it may bloom again. Divide and repot the fleshy rhizomes after blooming has stopped. New plant growth will follow soon. Flowering rush is cold hardy and can be left in the garden over winter.

Special notes
Flowering rush is a noxious weed in some regions. Check with your state department of natural resources before planting.

Forget-me-not
(*Myosotis palustris*)

A low-growing water garden favorite, forget-me-not rings in summer with dainty blue flowers. In climates with warm winters, grow it as a winter annual and enjoy color for months.

Where to plant

Plant forget-me-not in full sun or part shade. It grows well in moist soil or moving water such as near a waterfall or stream. Forget-me-not reaches 6 to 8 inches tall and spreads about 12 inches wide. It is hardy in Zones 5 to 9.

Growing

Plant forget-me-not in a shallow container filled with heavy garden soil. The plant often flowers intermittently throughout summer as long as it is cool. In warm humid climates it withers and leaves may turn dark. Trim wilted leaves; the plant will perk up when cooler days return. In southern climates, forget-me-not is best grown as a winter annual.

Special notes

'Mermaid' has large blue flowers with a white eye. 'Pinkie' forms a creeping cushion of cotton candy pink flowers. The pure white flowers of 'Snowflakes' open in spring and continue blooming through summer.

Foxtail
(*Myriophyllum heterophyllum*)

A hardy underwater favorite, foxtail stems can reach an impressive 6 feet long in large ponds. It grows well in containers. Beware, this vigorous plant can be invasive.

Where to plant

Foxtail does well in sun or shade. It grows 1 to 10 feet below the water surface and is a good choice for both inground and container water gardens. Foxtail is hardy in Zones 3 to 11.

Growing

Plant foxtail in a large, shallow container filled with sand or small gravel. The plant will slowly colonize to form a 1-foot-wide clump. The plant's thin, wispy leaves grow from a stout central stem and the foliage is dark reddish-brown and fluffy when submerged, somewhat like a fox's tail.

Foxtail grows vigorously. Regularly thin excessive clumps to prevent plants from overtaking the pond. Dispose of plants in a compost pile, and be sure they do not make their way to a local waterway.

Special notes

There are several similar species of foxtail including *M. hippuroides*. *M. spicatum*, water milfoil, is often sold but is highly invasive and prohibited in some states.

Hibiscus
(*Hibiscus* spp.)

Call on hibiscus for a bold burst of color along the edges of a water garden. This shrublike plant's large, colorful flowers unfurl and bloom for weeks in summer.

YOU SHOULD KNOW
The large flowers of hibiscus are favorites of butterflies and hummingbirds. Create a nectar buffet by planting several varieties throughout your water garden.

Where to plant
Hibiscus thrives in full sun or part shade. This easy-to-grow plant reaches 4 to 6 feet tall and 2 to 4 feet wide. It grows well in moist soil or submerged in water that is about 6 inches deep. Hibiscus is hardy in Zones 5 to 11.

Growing
Plant hibiscus in a shallow container filled with heavy garden soil. It dies back to the crown in winter and is slow to emerge in spring. In cold zones it commonly doesn't send up new stems until late spring. After the water and soil temperature have adequately warmed, it will send up new shoots.

Special notes
Hardy mallow (*H. moscheutos*) has stunning 10- to 12-inch flowers in colors ranging from white through deep red.

Highbush cranberry
(*Viburnum trilobum*)

Highbush cranberry is decorated with white flowers in spring followed by shiny red fruits that persist into winter. A large shrub, it makes a wonderful hedge.

Where to plant
Plant highbush cranberry in full sun or part shade. It grows well in a wide range of soils but prefers not to grow in standing water. Locate it near the edge of a rain garden, where it is less likely to be stressed by excessive moisture. Highbush cranberry grows 15 feet tall and about 4 to 6 feet wide with a pleasing rounded shape. It is hardy in Zones 2 to 7.

Growing
Water highbush cranberry regularly while it is establishing a strong root system. It requires little maintenance after that. Pruning, in early spring, is necessary only when the plant is overgrown. Highbush cranberry fruits are edible. Harvest them in late summer or fall for the sweetest flavor.

Special notes
Most highbush cranberries are sold simply as the species, but some cultivars are available. 'Wentworth', 'Andrew', and 'Hahs' are known for their high-quality fruit.

Hornwort
(Ceratophyllum demersum)

Resembling an underwater juniper bush, hornwort has dense, dark green foliage. Because of its dark foliage, it is rarely visible from the surface of the water.

Where to plant

Hornwort grows in sun or shade and at a depth of 1 to 10 feet below the water surface. Its stems will expand 10 feet or more, and a colony of hornwort will grow to be about 1 foot wide. It is hardy in Zones 5 to 11.

Growing

Hornwort does not produce roots, so there is no need for a pot or soil. Simply put it in the pond. If you would like to keep it in one place and at a certain depth, secure it to a brick with a rubber band. If hornwort becomes overly aggressive in your water feature, don't hesitate to remove entire clumps. It will quickly reestablish as long as a few plants are left in place.

Special notes

Hornwort makes an excellent spawning ground for fish in spring and is somewhat resistant to koi feeding. Because of its vigorous growth, it will quickly produce new stems if koi do nibble on it.

Houttuynia
(Houttuynia cordata 'Chameleon')

Plant low-growing houttuynia near a pond edge, where it will create a carpet of color around more upright growers such as cattail, flowering rush, and arrowhead.

Where to plant

Houttuynia grows well in sun or shade. It is a rampant grower and will quickly become invasive if not confined. Be sure to plant it in a container. Houttuynia grows 6 to 8 inches tall and spreads rapidly. It is hardy in Zones 5 to 11.

Growing

Plant houttuynia in a shallow container filled with heavy garden soil. White, single-petale flowers appear in late summer. Protect plants from freezing temperatures by submerging them in the pond.

Special notes

'Chameleon' has heart-shape leaves splashed with yellow and red. In fall the leaves turn dark maroon-purple. Double-flowering 'Plena' has small blooms that resemble rosebuds.

Iris (*Iris* spp.)

Just like their terrestrial counterparts, water-loving irises unfurl graceful flowers in spring and early summer. Their old-fashioned appeal lends any water garden a sense of permanence. Many different types of irises thrive in the moist soil and even submerged in the water in and around water gardens. These elegant tall plants are easy to grow and add valuable height and color to the garden.

Where to plant

Irises grow well in full sun or part shade. Some species grow best with water over their crowns throughout the year, even in fall and winter. These true water irises include yellow flag (*I. pseudacorus*), southern blue flag (*I. virginica*), blue flag (*I. versicolor*), rabbit-ear iris (*I. laevigata*), and some Louisiana irises.

Others tolerate wet soil for part of the growing season but prefer drier conditions. Japanese iris (*I. ensata*), Siberian iris (*I. sibirica*), and Rocky Mountain iris (*I. missouriensis*) grow well in the moist soil near pond and stream margins as well as in the dry conditions of a perennial garden. Irises also grow well in container water gardens.

Irises grow 2 to 4 feet tall and spread 1 to 2 feet wide. Hardiness varies by cultivar. Most irses are hardy in Zones 3 to 9.

Growing

Grow water irises in pots set into the pond. Fill the pot three-fourths full of heavy garden soil, and place the rhizome in the center with its cut end toward the edge of the container. Next, fill the pot with soil, leaving about 1 inch of space between the soil and the pot rim. Spread a ½-inch layer of pea gravel over the soil. Water the container well and set it in the water garden.

Japanese, Siberian, and Rocky Mountain irises all grow well when planted at the pond edge. Plant the rhizomes shallowly so they are about an inch or so below the soil surface.

Divide and transplant irises immediately after they finish flowering.

Allow iris foliage to stand during winter. Some species develop a pleasing auburn hue that adds color and texture to the winter garden. In early spring, cut the foliage back to ground level.

Special notes

Louisiana irises grow well in almost any climate. Water depth needed depends on the iris's ancestry; if you're not sure how deep to plant it, situate the rhizome just below the water's surface. Louisiana irises are rampant growers and should be potted when used in a pond. Their spectacular flowers, which come in a wide variety of colors, bloom best in full sun.

Yellow flag iris owes its name to its bright yellow flowers in early spring. Growing as tall as 4 feet, it is suitable for large ponds.

Both **blue flag and southern blue flag** have light blue flowers in midspring, and their blue-green sword-shape leaves take on a dark red stain from the base to the tips.

Rabbit-ear iris has short, rounded but upright petals on white, elegant blue, or royal reddish-purple blooms. In areas with cool summers, it usually grows only 12 to 19 inches tall; it'll grow 2 to 3 feet tall elsewhere. Also called Japanese water iris, rabbit-ear iris has flowers 6 inches or more in diameter. Blossoms colors range from velvety deep purple to the cleanest white.

Siberian iris works well in the bog garden or in moist areas of the perennial garden—close to but not submerged in water—and do best in full sun. They are hardy in many climates, and their flowers bloom in late spring or early summer. Hybrids are available in white and yellow, but most types bear two or three dark-veined purple flowers on each stem.

For the most part, irises bridge the seasons of spring and summer, adding color during the transition. They have strongly upright foliage that fits a formal setting and adds structure to an informal cottage-style garden.

varieties

① **'ROSE ADAGIO'** is a striking variety of rabbit-ear iris with a lovely purple-red edge on its slightly ruffled petals.

② **'DARK LIGHTNING'** rabbit-ear iris illustrates the wide variety of colors within this group of iris. The bold combination of deep purple and yellow make an eye-catching statement.

③ **SIBERIAN IRISES** often have smaller flowers than rabbit-ear iris. Their striking upright foliage sways in the wind and turns auburn in fall.

Jack-in-the-pulpit
(*Arisaema triphyllum*)

A woodland native, jack-in-the-pulpit bursts into blossom in midspring when much of the garden is slowly waking up from a long winter. It is superb in rain gardens.

Where to plant

Jack-in-the-pulpit grows best in moist to well-drained soil and part or full shade. Plant it in the shade of trees and shrubs in the rain garden. It is hardy in Zones 3 to 8.

Growing

Purchase 1- to 2-foot-tall jack-in-the-pulpit from specialty garden centers or mail order plant suppliers. Do not collect plants from the wild. Jack-in-the-pulpit grows best in soil that is rich in organic matter. Before planting incorporate a generous amount of compost into the growing area. Plant container-grown plants in early spring, and water them well until the young plants establish a strong root system.

After plants become established in a favorable site, they will likely self-seed. Excess seedlings are easy to eradicate by hoeing.

Special notes

This perennial's striking flowers are followed by clusters of bright red berries. The berries, along with all other parts of the plant, are toxic.

Joe-pye weed
(*Eupatorium maculatum*)

The mauve blossoms atop the stately burgundy stems of joe-pye weed beckon butterflies and bees. This large perennial is great for adding height to a rain garden.

Where to plant

Plant joe-pye weed in full sun or part shade and moist soil. It grows especially well in soil that is enriched with compost. Joe-pye weed grows an impressive 4 to 6 feet tall and about 4 feet wide. Its sturdy stems don't usually need staking. It is hardy in Zones 3 to 9.

Growing

Water plants well after transplanting. Pinch off the top 3 or 4 inches of growth from stems once or twice prior to July 4 to increase branching and flower number—and reduce final height.

Flowers form flat clusters 10 to 12 inches across. To prevent self-sowing, deadhead plants before windborne seeds ripen. Powdery mildew can attack plants; thin the stems to improve air circulation. Divide plants in spring.

Special notes

'Gateway' is a compact form of joe-pye weed, growing about 5 feet tall. It is especially striking when paired with tall ornamental grasses.

Lizard's tail
(*Saururus* spp.)

The nodding white blooms of lizard's tail last all summer. Use this 1- to 3-foot-tall plant as a living screen at the far edge of your pond or stream.

Where to plant

Lizard's tail grows in full sun or part shade. The plant's heart-shape leaves and white, arching flower spikes stand tall on 1- to 3-foot stems. Lizard's tail will grow in moist soil or when submerged in 6 inches of water. It is hardy in Zones 4 to 11.

Growing

Plant lizard's tail in a shallow container filled with heavy garden soil. The plant will quickly form a dense colony of stems.

Although lizard's tail will withstand frost, it cannot tolerate being frozen in the pond. In fall move it to a deep part of the pond so its rhizomes won't freeze during winter.

Special notes

Common lizard's tail (*S. cernuus*) has white flowers lasting from June through frost.

Chinese lizard's tail (*S. chinensis*) has a white splotch on the topmost leaf, making the plant ornamental even when not in flower.

Lobelia
(*Lobelia* spp.)

A favorite of hummingbirds and butterflies, lobelia is beloved for its brilliant flowers, which appear in summer through fall. Grow lobelia in water and perennial gardens.

Where to plant

Lobelia grows well in full sun or part shade but flowers most prolifically in full sun. This hardy perennial grows 6 inches to 5 feet tall depending on the species. Flower color varies from bright red or bright blue through crimson and purple. Lobelia grows best in moist soil at the edge of a water garden. It is hardy in Zones 5 to 11.

Growing

Plant lobelia in moist soil at the edge of a pond or stream. Although hardy, plants overwinter best when covered with a 3- to 4-inch-thick layer of mulch or submerged in a deep part of a water feature that does not freeze.

Special notes

Two of the most common lobelias are cardinal flower (*L. cardinalis*) and great blue lobelia (*L. siphilitica*). Cardinal flower has bright crimson flowers July through September on 3-foot-tall stems. Great blue lobelia is similar to cardinal flower in form and habit, with bright blue blossoms July through October.

YOU SHOULD KNOW
Brush against the flowers and leaves of lizard's tail and you'll find that they are aromatic, with a fragrance similar to vanilla. Other fragrant water plants include hardy and tropical water lilies as well as lotuses.

Lotus *(Nelumbo* spp.)

An ancient plant, lotus has been prized for thousands of years for its graceful, fragrant blossoms that rise above magnificent round, waxy leaves. Its long-lasting seedpods are intriguing too. Recent plant breeding work has yielded plants that thrive in small container gardens as well as those that grow with abandon in large ponds. Choose your favorite cultivar of this much-loved plant and enjoy its beauty in your own water garden.

Where to plant

Lotuses are sun-loving plants, and most cultivars require six hours of direct sunlight a day to produce blooms. Although not tropical plants, they love hot weather, preferring warm soil and water temperatures. They grow well in shallow water and bogs. When planting them in standing water, situate the pots so the crown, or growing point, is about 1 foot below the water surface. Large varieties will tolerate deeper water. Lotuses are hardy in Zones 4 to 11.

Growing

Lotuses produce a series of vigorous underground stems called rhizomes. The rhizomes have growth points at the joints where aboveground stems and leaves emerge. Plant a lotus in the largest container possible to promote maximum production of stems and flowers.

To pot a lotus, first fill a large container half full with heavy garden soil. Add slow-release fertilizer according to package directions—aquatic fertilizer tablets are easiest to use. Add soil to the container until the soil level is 4 inches below the top of the pot. Make a slight depression in the soil. Gently place the lotus rhizome in the depression. Cover the thickest part with 2 inches of soil, keeping the growing tip ½ inch above the soil. Gently place a flat rock on the covered section of the rhizome. Carefully spread ½ inch of pea gravel over the soil surface, being careful not to cover the growing tip. Water the newly planted lotus well. Slowly lower the pot into the water.

Lotuses generally do not start growing until the water reaches 60°F in spring. They bloom several weeks later than water lilies and require several weeks of temperatures in the 80s to bloom. In cold zones expect lotuses to flower for six to eight weeks beginning in late July or August. In areas where days are warm and nights are cold, cover lotuses with a protective plastic canopy to retain warmth overnight.

Lotuses are hardy water plants that can be overwintered even in cold climates. Cut back the foliage to the water surface after the leaves have died and turned brown. If you cut back the leaves while still green, fungal or bacterial infections can reach the rhizome and kill the plant.

Overwinter lotuses as you would hardy water lilies, keeping the rhizomes deep enough in the pond that ice and frost will not reach them. If you do not overwinter your lotus in your pond, put the pot in a plastic bag and store it where it will stay cool (but not freezing), dark, and damp.

Special notes

There are two species of lotus—American lotus (*N. lutea*) and Asian lotus (*N. nucifera*). American lotus has creamy yellow flowers usually with a single ring of petals. Asian lotus has showy single, semidouble, or fully double blooms in shades of white and pink.

Lotus cultivars are available in a wide range of sizes and colors. Some selections are truly miniature, growing no more than a foot or so in height with flowers no larger than a daisy. Others are huge and stately, standing more than 6 feet tall, with leaves more than 2 feet in diameter and flowers as large as basketballs. Fragrance varies from heady and fruity to mild, like baby powder. Colors range from the deepest rosy pink to the cleanest white.

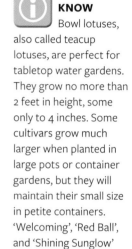

YOU SHOULD KNOW
Bowl lotuses, also called teacup lotuses, are perfect for tabletop water gardens. They grow no more than 2 feet in height, some only to 4 inches. Some cultivars grow much larger when planted in large pots or container gardens, but they will maintain their small size in petite containers. 'Welcoming', 'Red Ball', and 'Shining Sunglow' grow to 1 foot or so tall.

varieties

1. **'MRS. PERRY D. SLOCUM'** has 9- to 12-inch double blossoms with an intoxicating fragrance. Flowers open deep pink and change to creamy yellow. It stands 4 to 5 feet tall. Best for large ponds.
2. **'BABY DOLL'** is a free-flowering lotus that is ideal for container water gardens. It grows 2 to 3 feet tall. When grown in full sun, it flowers vigorously, with as many as a dozen white flowers at one time.
3. **'CHAWAN BASU'** is a dwarf lotus with white flowers tinged with pink. Flowers unfurl 5 to 9 inches across. It is a good choice for container gardens and small ponds.
4. **'MOMO BOTAN'** grows 1 to 2 feet tall and has very fragrant large pink flowers that measure 4 to 10 inches across. This small cultivar grows well in containers and small ponds.

Marsh betony
(*Stachys palustris*)

Purple or pink snapdragon-like flowers decorate marsh betony from summer to fall. It finishes the season in style when its leaves turn bright yellow.

Where to plant

Marsh betony grows well in sun or shade. The plant grows 6 to 24 inches tall and spreads by underground stems. It succeeds in moist soil or when submerged 5 inches below the water surface. Marsh betony is hardy in Zones 4 to 8.

Growing

Plant marsh betony in a shallow container filled with heavy garden soil. The plant spreads by runners and is best confined in a container, even when planted in a bog. The bright green leaves turn bright yellow in fall, adding interest to the autumn water garden.

Divide marsh betony in early spring when it first starts to sprout. Perfectly winter hardy, the plant requires no special care or treatment to survive freezing weather.

Special notes

Marsh betony is a welcome substitute for noxious purple loosestrife (*Lythrum* spp.), a prohibited weed that chokes out wetlands.

Marsh marigold
(*Caltha palustris*)

One of the earliest blooming water garden plants, marsh marigold has sunny yellow flowers atop a tidy clump of cool green foliage. It grows well at the water's edge.

Where to plant

Marsh marigold grows and blooms best in full sun or part shade. It forms a mound 12 to 18 inches tall and wide. It is hardy in Zones 4 to 7.

Growing

Plant marsh marigold in moist garden soil at the edge of a pond or stream. Or plant it in a shallow container filled with heavy soil and submerge the container 1 inch below the water surface.

In cool climates marsh marigold grows from spring through fall, blooming on and off throughout the growing season. In warm areas it may die back in the hot summer sun.

Special notes

Also called water cowslip, marsh marigold has long been used medicinally but is poisonous if eaten raw.

ⓘ YOU SHOULD KNOW

Marsh marigold is related to a plant with a very similar name—floating marsh marigold (*Caltha natans*). Both plants bloom in spring, adding welcome color to the water garden. Add more early spring color by planting easy-care flowering shrubs such as forsythia, quince, azaleas, rhododendrons, and lilacs to the well-drained soil near your water feature.

Parrot's feather
(*Myriophyllum aquaticum*)

Whorls of feathery foliage are the hallmarks of parrot's feather. The foliage floats gracefully on the water surface and is a great complement to glossy water lily pads.

Where to plant

Parrot's feather succeeds in full sun or part shade. This vigorous plant grows 6 inches tall and spreads rapidly by runners. It will thrive in moist soil or simply floating in water. The plant is hardy in Zones 6 to 11.

Growing

Plant parrot's feather in a shallow container filled with heavy garden soil. It can also be grown as a floating plant.

The plant may survive a winter freeze if submerged beneath the water, but it is not reliably hardy in cold areas. To ensure survival, cut a 6-inch piece of stem in early fall. Submerge the cut end in a glass of water and place it in a sunny window. The stem will produce roots in a few weeks. Overwinter it in the glass.

Special notes

Because parrot's feather grows rampantly, it has earned a place on the prohibited noxious weed list in some states. Before buying plants, check with your state department of natural resources to ensure that it is allowed in your state.

Pickerel weed
(*Pontederia cordata*)

Dragonflies, butterflies, and hummingbirds flock to pickerel weed's nectar-rich, attractive white or purple flower spikes, which last for weeks in summer.

Where to plant

Pickerel weed, also called pickerel plant and pickerel rush, grows well in full sun or part shade. It reaches 24 to 30 inches tall and spreads 12 to 18 inches wide. Pickerel weed is easy to grow and tolerates moist soil or being submerged up to 10 inches below the water surface. It is hardy in Zones 5 to 11.

Growing

Plant pickerel weed in moist soil at the edge of a pond or stream or in a bog garden. Or plant it in a shallow container filled with heavy garden soil and place it in the pond.

For best overwintering ability, buy plants that have been grown for the climate in which you will raise them. In cold climates protect roots from freezing. Place the plants well below the frost line of the pond or remove the plants and store them in a cold, damp area until spring.

Special notes

'White Pike' has flowers that are white rather than purple. 'Pink Pons' has lavender-pink flowers.

Red ludwigia
(*Ludwigia glandulosa*)

True to its name, red ludwigia adds a splash of red to the water garden. The intensity of its red-green leaves depends on the water quality and sun exposure.

Where to plant

Red ludwigia grows best and develops more intense coloring in full sun. Plants grown in shade will have mostly green foliage. Unlike the red foliage, which is visible from above, the green foliage blends into the pond water. Red ludwigia is hardy in Zones 4 to 10.

Growing

Plant fast-growing red ludwiga in a large shallow container filled with sand or small gravel. The plant's creeping runners will expand slowly to form a colony. Its leaves will sometimes extend above the water surface.

Red ludwigia adds striking color to container gardens. Add a couple stems to your next potted aquatic garden.

Special notes

Red ludwigia can also be grown as a floating plant. Simply place rooted cuttings in the water and they will form a floating colony.

Rose turtlehead
(*Chelone obliqua*)

In the rain garden or a moist spot, rose turtlehead's spikes of small, deep rose-purple blooms in late summer and fall add beauty as well as attract wildlife.

Where to plant

Rose turtlehead grows well in dense shade and moist soil. It tolerates heavy clay along with full sun, provided the soil is constantly moist. The plant is hardy in Zones 4 to 10.

Growing

Rose turtlehead grows 2 to 3 feet tall and 1 foot wide. It spreads by shallow rhizomes, forming wide, dense colonies. Layer a planting with 1 to 2 inches of compost in fall to renew its vigor.

Special notes

Butterflies, bees, and hummingbirds flock to rose turtlehead's flower spikes. The blossoms are especially important because they serve as a food source late into the fall.

Rose turtlehead has glossy foliage and a strong vertical form. Pair it with hosta, astilbe, or sensitive fern in a moist, shady spot. 'Hot Lips' is a short variety of the closely related pink turtlehead (*C. lyonii*).

Rush

(*Juncus* spp. and *Scirpus* spp.)

These stiff, upright grasslike plants are a perfect complement to water lilies, lotuses, and other favorite flowering water plants. Capitalize on rush's strong architecture by positioning it among low-growing plants. It will quickly become a focal point. Thanks to its evergreen nature, it will add valuable interest to the water garden year-round.

Where to plant

Grow rushes in full sun or part shade. Most are noted for their long spiked stems, which are usually dark green but can be light blue. The stems typically grow 2 to 3 feet tall and spread about 2 feet wide. Rushes grow well in moist soil or when submerged 4 to 6 inches below the water surface. They are hardy in Zones 4 to 9.

Growing

Plant in moist soil near the edge of a pond or stream or in a bog. Rushes will also grow well in a shallow container filled with heavy garden soil and submerged in the pond. With adequate moisture, they grow well in a perennial border.

In many climates rushes are evergreen. Cut them back to the ground occasionally to remove older, tattered growth.

Rush plants grow from underground rhizomes that are easy to divide. Divide plants in early spring just after they begin growing.

Most rushes are cold tolerant and may be overwintered in the pond. Move container-planted rushes to an area of the pond that doesn't freeze during winter. Overwinter tender species, such as Australian silver rush (*J. polyanthemos*) indoors and treat them as houseplants.

Special notes

Soft rush (*J. effusus*), below left, has stiff spines of green foliage. It often retains its color all year, even in cold climates. Corkscrew rush (*J. effusus* 'Spiralis'), *below right*, has tightly coiled foliage, which adds lovely texture to the water garden. It is almost evergreen, even in cold climates. 'Gold Strike' has dark green leaves accented with gold stripes along their length.

Blue rush (*J. inflexus*) has baby blue foliage resembling that of blue fescue. It grows in full sun and takes moist soil to 2-inch-deep water. They plant is hardy to Zone 4.

Woolly rush (*Scirpus cyperinus*) is distinguished by its fluffy silken tassels of tawny brown at the end of stiff dark green foliage. It forms a dense clump. Many plants in the genus *Scirpus* have a tendency to spread vigorously, much more than those in *Juncus*.

YOU SHOULD KNOW
Rush plants provide important shelter for fish, fowl, and insects. Dragonfly larvae often use the upright leaves to climb out of the water, clinging to the stiff foliage for camouflage while they metamorphose into adult dragonflies.

Sedge
(*Carex* spp.)

Sedge's tufted clump of grasslike foliage is at home in all kinds of water gardens—from tabletop gardens to ponds. Plant it at the edge of the garden.

YOU SHOULD KNOW When transplanting sedge, keep plants well watered until roots form. Once sedges are established, they typically need watering only during the driest part of the growing season, in peak summer.

Where to plant

Plant sedge in sun or shade. Most varieties grow 6 to 12 inches tall and wide. Plants will grow in moist soil or submerged up to 1 inch below the water surface. Sedge is hardy in Zones 4 to 11.

Growing

Sedge belongs in the moist soil near a pond or stream. It will also grow well in a bog garden. To grow sedge in water, plant it in a shallow container filled with heavy garden soil. Submerge the container in shallow water.

Divide sedge in early spring. Most varieties are winter hardy and will overwinter well in the pond or in moist soil at the water's edge. For extra winter protection, spread a 2-inch-thick layer of mulch over plants that are not growing in a pond or stream.

Special notes

Blue sedge (*C. flacca*) has striking frosty blue foliage. Inflated tassel sedge (*C. fascicularis*) has puffy seedheads that resemble spiny cucumbers.

Serviceberry
(*Amelanchier laevis*)

A water-loving shrub or small tree, serviceberry has white flowers in spring, berries that beckon birds in early summer, and bright orange-red fall foliage color.

Where to plant

Serviceberry grows well in full sun or part shade. It will tolerate less sun than many other shrubs. It grows well with as little as four hours of sun a day. Serviceberry grows 15 to 25 feet tall and has a rounded shape. Limit the lofty height of this native shrub by pruning it regularly. You can easily train it into a multistemmed tree form. It is hardy in Zones 3 to 8.

Growing

After planting, water serviceberry regularly until it establishes a strong root system. Prune the plant in spring after it blooms.

Serviceberry produces numerous stems to form a sprawling colony. Limit its spread by cutting these suckering branches back to ground level in early spring.

Special notes

'Cumulus' has a broadly columnar habit, unlike the sometimes sprawling, rounded habit of the species. It has orange autumn foliage.

Snowberry
(*Symphoricarpos albus*)

Aptly named, snowberry has berrylike white fruits from September through November. Its green foliage and pleasing round form are valuable assets during spring and summer.

Where to plant

Snowberry grows well in full sun or part shade. Aim to provide it with at least six hours of sun per day. This shrub thrives in moist soil but will tolerate short periods of droughty conditions. It grows 3 to 6 feet tall and has a round habit. The plant is hardy in Zones 3 to 7.

Growing

After planting, water snowberry regularly to promote a strong root system. Prune as needed in early spring. Snowberry tends to produce suckering stems; cut it back to the ground in early spring to limit the shrub's spread.

Special notes

Snowberry's green foliage is useful for providing a simple backdrop alongside flowering perennials such as black-eyed susan and joe-pye weed in the rain garden. When the perennials are done flowering, snowberry will add interest with its white berries.

Swamp milkweed
(*Asclepias incarnata*)

This fragrant pink wildflower blooms summer through fall. Butterflies flock to the flowers to sip nectar and the monarch butterfly larvae feeds on its leaves.

Where to plant

Plant swamp milkweed in full sun. It thrives in moist soil and will grow well in the wettest part of the rain garden. Its tall, sometimes arching stems reach 6 feet. It is hardy in Zones 3 to 9.

Growing

After planting, water swamp milkweed well so it establishes a strong root system. Swamp milkweed is easy to grow and will tolerate moist, boggy soil for days at a time.

Promote rebloom by deadheading plants after they bloom. Allow the foliage and flowers to stand during winter to serve as shelter for birds. In spring cut the foliage back to ground level.

Divide swamp milkweed in early spring, replanting divisions where they have plenty of space to spread.

Special notes

'Ice Ballet' has white flowers and 3-foot-tall stems. 'Cinderella' has rose pink blooms on 3- to 5-foot-tall stems. Butterfly weed (*A. tuberosa*) is a popular nectar source for butterflies. It grows best in well-drained soil.

Sweet flag
(*Acorus calamus*)

Tidy sweet flag is invaluable for adding textural interest to a water garden. For a splash of color, too, choose a variegated selection of this easy-to-grow perennial.

Where to plant

Sweet flag grows well in sun or shade. It is an aquatic plant that will tolerate shade. Depending on the cultivar, the thin, grasslike leaves grow 8 to 36 inches tall and the plant spreads about 18 inches wide. Sweet flag thrives in moist soil or submerged up to 6 inches below the water surface. It is hardy in Zones 4 to 11.

Growing

Plant sweet flag in moist soil near the edge of a water garden or in a bog. To grow it in the water, plant it in a shallow container filled with heavy garden soil.

Sweet flag can overwinter in the pond or in a mulched perennial border, but don't let it dry out. Water deeply in fall.

Special notes

Sweet flag (*A. calamus*), green and variegated forms, are tall and upright. They grow from roots that run freely and form small clumps. Graceful 'Ogon' Japanese sweet flag (*A. gramineus*) has light green foliage with bright yellow stripes and is generally evergreen.

Switch grass
(*Panicum virgatum*)

The fine-texture foliage of switch grass adds elegance to the rain garden. This ornamental grass develops pretty fall color before turning tan in winter.

Where to plant

Switch grass grows well in full sun or part shade. It forms a narrow, upright clump 5 feet tall and 2 feet wide. The plant tolerates moist soil and will withstand drought as well. It is hardy in Zones 3 to 9.

Growing

Switch grass is very easy to grow. After planting, water it well so it establishes a strong root system before winter.

Use switch grass as a living screen by planting a row of six to nine plants along one side of the rain garden. Its gauzy white blooms open in mid- to late summer. In fall allow the tan stems to remain in the garden, providing winter interest.

Special notes

'Cloud Nine' has slender icy blue leaves and clouds of rust-color blooms. It grows 6 feet tall. 'Dallas Blues' develops drooping pale blue leaves. Huge rosy-purple seedheads ripen to tan in fall. 'Heavy Metal' has powder blue leaves that turn yellow in fall.

YOU SHOULD KNOW Small forms of sweet flag are prone to spider mites. Large selections may develop a fungus that causes black spots and can kill the foliage. Clean up dead foliage in autumn. Remove affected leaves if spots appear.

Taro
(*Colocasia esculenta*)

Count on taro to make a bold splash of color and texture in the water garden. It is well suited to large water features as well as container water gardens.

Where to plant
Plant taro, also called elephant's ear, in full sun or part shade. Its massive arrow-shape leaves come in many beautiful colors. It grows 2 to 6 feet tall and spreads 2 to 4 feet wide. Tolerant of moist soil or standing water, taro grows well in bogs and wet soil or submerged up to 6 inches below the water surface. Taro is hardy in Zones 10 to 11.

Growing
Plant taro in moist soil at the edge of a pond or stream or in a bog garden. If submerging taro, first plant it in a shallow container filled with heavy garden soil before placing it in the water.

Overwinter plants indoors by keeping the pots in saucers of water in a warm, sunny room. Or let the plants dry out; then dig up the corms (root structures) and store them until spring in coarse vermiculite in a cool, dark spot.

Special notes
'Black Magic' taro has black-purple leaves and stems. 'Metallica' is particularly elegant, with deep purple stems and velvety blue-green leaves.

Thalia
(*Thalia* spp.)

Thalia's clump of lush green foliage lends a pronounced tropical look to any water garden. It bears silvery purple flowers that droop from long arching stems in summer.

Where to plant
Thalia, also called alligator flag, grows well in full sun or part shade. It has striking leaves that can reach 2 feet wide and more than 3 feet long. Plants grow 4 to 8 feet tall. Thalia grows well in moist soil or submerged up to 1 foot below the water surface. It is hardy in Zones 5 to 11.

Growing
Plant thalia in moist soil at the edge of a pond or stream or in a bog garden. To grow it in standing water, plant it in a shallow container filled with heavy garden soil. In winter, cover plants growing in moist soil with a 4- to 5-inch-thick layer of mulch for added protection. Move submerged plants to a deep area of the pond where they will not freeze.

Special notes
Purple thalia (*T. dealbata*) overwinters in cold climates without protection. Blue Cup Leaf Form purple thalia has blue leaves that are more cup shape than others. Broad Leafed Form has flat leaves that are triangular. The foliage looks tropical and has a slightly powder blue color.

Umbrella grass
(*Cyperus* spp.)

Also called cyperus, umbrella grass is grown for its lovely sprays of ornamental leaf fronds. There's a species of umbrella grass—from very large to very small—for every pond.

Where to plant

Umbrella grass grows best in full sun or part shade. Its preferred water depth varies by species, ranging from moist soil to sitting in several inches of water. Most types are hardy in Zones 9 to 11.

Growing

Plant umbrella grass in a shallow container filled with heavy garden soil. All species are heavy feeders and should be fertilized once a month. Only a few species are hardy in cold regions, but plants will overwinter easily in a cool, moist, sunny window or other light-filled location.

Special notes

Umbrella grass (*C. alternifolius*) is the most commonly sold species. Its uppermost leaf sprout can grow up to 2 feet in diameter. Individual leaves are about ½ inch wide and 1 foot or more in length. A quick grower, umbrella grass usually requires division every few years.

Dwarf umbrella grass (*C. involucratus* 'Nanus') is a 2-foot-tall plant with long umbrella-like fronds. It is hardy in Zones 9 to 11.

Variegated water celery
(*Oenanthe javanica* 'Flamingo')

The leaves of this low-growing water plant are edible—they have a peppery flavor and are tasty added to salads.

Where to plant

Variegated water celery grows well in sun or shade, but develops the most intense coloring when it is planted in full sun or part shade. It grows 6 to 12 inches tall and has frilly white, pink, and green foliage that resembles a carrot top. The plant is hardy in Zones 5 to 11.

Growing

Plant variegated water celery along the edge of a pond, stream, or waterfall or in a large container water garden. It produces running stems and will form a colony of colorful foliage. Variegated water celery winters easily in cold climates and withstands freezing.

Special notes

Also called water parsley, water celery plants are excellent filters. They take up nutrients that would otherwise contribute to algae formation.

Water bluebell
(Ruellia brittoniana)

The petunia of the water garden, water bluebell is covered with large flowers for months in summer. Plant it along the pond edge, where it will create a carpet of color.

Where to plant

Water bluebell grows well in full sun or part shade. Its 1- to 2-inch-wide flowers will decorate the pond edge or shallow regions in the water garden. It grows well in moist soil or in water up to 6 inches deep. It is hardy in Zones 9 to 11.

Growing

Plant water bluebell in the moist soil along the edge of a water feature or in a container filled with heavy garden soil and placed in shallow water.

Water bluebell blooms best in tropical climates, where it is blanketed with flowers for months during summer. In cold climates the foliage often turns a lovely dark purple when night temperatures cool. Because plants do not withstand cold temperatures, they must be wintered indoors as houseplants.

Special notes

The species is very easy to grow. 'Chi Chi' is a delightful pink variation with foliage that turns burgundy in fall. Dwarf 'Katie' has blue flowers that nestle tightly against the stems.

Water canna
(Canna spp.)

Canna's bold foliage and flashy yellow, red, or orange flowers are sure to catch your eye. Plants grow several feet tall and bloom with gusto until frost.

Where to plant

Cannas grow well in full sun or part shade. They bloom best when they receive at least six hours of bright sun a day. Water cannas (*C. glauca* and *C. flaccida*) grow well in saturated soil with water over their crowns. Other cannas are terrestrial but will adapt to waterlogged soil. Water cannas are hardy in Zones 9 to 11; other cannas are hardy in Zones 7 to 11.

Growing

Plant cannas in moist soil at the edge of a pond or stream or in a bog garden. To grow a canna in standing water, plant the rhizome in a shallow container filled with heavy garden soil.

Dig up the rhizomes, remove the foliage, and let them dry outdoors for a few days before bringing them indoors for the winter. Store them in a cool, dark spot until spring.

Special notes

There are hundreds of varieties of cannas. Canna foliage varies in color from bright green to blue-green, dark purple, or crimson to green striped in yellow, white, or red.

YOU SHOULD KNOW Canna rhizomes can be tricky to plant. When dormant, they are brown, potato-like roots. You might wonder how to situate them in the soil. Look for the pink or green growth point called the bud. Stems and leaves will emerge from this point. Plant the rhizome so the bud is on top.

Water clover
(*Marsilea* spp.)

The lucky charm of the water garden, this low-growing plant forms a lovely green cover on the water surface or when growing in the soil nearby.

Where to plant

Water clover grows well in sun or shade and does best in shallow water that is rather still. It grows about 6 inches tall and spreads to form a dense mat. Plant it in moist soil or submerged up to 4 inches below the water surface. Water clover is hardy in Zones 5 to 11.

Growing

Plant water clover at the edge of a pond or stream or in a bog garden. To grow it in standing water, plant it in a shallow container filled with heavy garden soil. Water clover is easy to overwinter in cold climates, provided the soil it is growing in does not freeze. Place plants on the bottom of the pond with other frost-intolerant aquatics such as hardy water lilies and lotuses.

Special notes

Most species of water clover have foliage that emerges above the water surface. The leaves of floating water clover (*M. mutica*) float on the water. The emerged leaves open in the morning. When they close at night, they look like small butterflies at rest.

Water horsetail
(*Equisetum fluviatile*)

Water horsetail's stiff, upright stems make a pleasing sound when the wind whistles through them. Be sure to grow this vigorous plant in a pot where its spread can be contained.

Where to plant

Water horsetail grows well in sun or shade. It stands about 2 feet tall and will spread to form a large clump. It grows well in moist soil or submerged 6 to 12 inches below the water surface. It is hardy in Zones 4 to 11.

Growing

Plant water horsetail in moist soil near the edge of a pond or stream. It will also grow in a bog. Cold-tolerant horsetail survives winter at the pond edge.

To contain its vigorous roots, plant water horsetail in a shallow container filled with heavy garden soil. To overwinter plants growing in standing water, submerge them in a deep area of the pond where they will not freeze.

Special notes

A North American native, water horsetail is also called scouring rush because of its usefulness in scrubbing pots and pans.

Water hyacinth
(*Eichhornia crassipes*)

Grown for its lavender flowers and spongy, round, shiny green foliage, this floating plant filters water so well that it is sometimes grown to treat sewage.

Where to plant
Water hyacinth grows well in sun or shade. It makes an ideal container plant; drop it in any pot that holds water. It also thrives in moving water. The plant will grow to 12 to 15 inches tall when crowded. Water hyacinth is hardy in Zones 9 to 11.

Growing
Water hyacinth grows best in warm water and won't survive freezing weather. Wait until the water is consistently above 65°F before planting. In cold climates, treat it like an annual. Be sure to remove plants prior to the first frost to prevent decaying foliage from collecting in the pond during winter.

Special notes
It is illegal to possess water hyacinth in some states, and federal law prohibits interstate commerce of it. Anchored water hyacinth (*E. azurea*) grows from a thick, fleshy stem that spreads across the water surface.

Water lettuce
(*Pistia stratiotes*)

Easy-to-grow water lettuce has spongy, velvety, lime-green foliage that grows in a pretty rosette resembling a floating clump of lush lettuce.

Where to plant
Water lettuce grows well in part shade and moving water. It will grow well in full sun and still water as well. Mature plants reach diameters of 15 to 20 inches when in a nutrient-rich environment. Water lettuce grows 4 to 12 inches tall. It is hardy in Zones 9 to 11.

Growing
Plant water lettuce when the water reaches 65°F. Remove plants prior to the first frost to keep decaying matter from collecting in the pond during winter.

Special notes
'Ruffles' grows 4 to 6 inches in diameter and has smaller leaves, with folds obscuring the center. 'Aqua Velvet' grows 6 to 8 inches wide and has deep blue-green leaves. 'Angio Splash' grows 6 to 8 inches across and is streaked and blotched in creamy yellow.

 YOU SHOULD KNOW Beware of invasives. Nearly all submerged and floating plants are considered to be invasive weeds in some locales. Individual species may even be banned in certain areas. Check with your state department of natural resources for regulations and guidelines on planting and propagating the ones you want to grow in your pond.

Water lily (*Nymphaea* spp.)

The striking beauty of pristine water lily petals and neatly formed flowers inspires many people to build their first water garden or create a container oasis for their patio or deck. Water lily cultivars are available in a multitude of flower and leaf colors and sizes, making it possible to find the perfect plants for your garden.

Where to plant

There are two types of water lilies—hardy water lilies and tropical water lilies. They differ in several ways. In general, as their names indicate, hardy water lilies will overwinter in cold zones, while tropical water lilies are tender and will not overwinter in areas where the water freezes. The following pages detail additional characteristics of the two groups of plants.

Water lilies grow best in full sun. Some cultivars, especially tropical water lilies, grow well in partial shade. The blazing afternoon sun in Zones 7 and higher necessitates a few hours of afternoon shade for some water lilies to prevent leaves from scorching and to promote blooms. Learn more about the sun requirements of individual water lilies by reading plant labels and researching the cultivar before planting.

Water lilies grow well submerged 6 to 36 inches below the water surface. Some varieties tolerate even deeper water, thriving at as much as 8 feet below the water surface.

Growing

Water lilies are easy to plant when they are small. Planting methods depend on whether they are hardy or tropical lilies. Hardy water lilies can be planted when they are dormant, when they have few or no leaves, or when they are in active growth, with roots and leaves that have already sprouted. Tropicals are generally shipped—and planted—in full active growth.

If you buy water lilies from a specialty water garden plant retailer—such as an online or mail order source—expect the plants to arrive bare-root, or without soil. They will resemble a cluster of roots and may include a rhizome or two. Don't despair. Although the plants look less than stellar, they are likely in prime condition for planting and growth.

Whether you are planting hardy or tropical water lilies, the general process is as follows. For planting tips specific to hardy and tropical water lilies, see pages 206 and 208.

Begin by choosing a planting container. Water lilies thrive when they have plenty of space for their root systems to expand. Choose a pot that is at least 17 inches wide and about 7 to 10 inches deep. Mesh water garden containers and recycled black plastic nursery pots work well.

Fill the container three-fourths full with heavy garden soil. Add slow-release fertilizer or fertilizer tabs specially designed for use with aquatic plants. Place the bare-root water lily in the pot and gently add soil around the roots. Be sure to keep the crown, or growing point, free of soil. Water the pot thoroughly and then top the soil with a ½-inch layer of pea gravel, again avoiding the plant's crown. Slowly lower the water lily into the water garden until 6 to 30 inches of water covers the pot.

Sit back and wait. Water lilies typically do not begin actively growing until two to four weeks after they are transplanted. Water lilies grow best when fertilized every month or so. For best bloom, use an aquatic plant fertilizer tab and follow label directions.

Special notes

Water lilies are often described as being suitable for small, medium, or large ponds. Choosing the right size water lily for your water garden is essential for a good bloom show. For container gardens, choose water lilies that grow 1 to 3 feet wide. A small pond can support water lilies that grow 3 to 6 feet wide. Medium ponds are well suited for water lilies that grow 6 to 10 feet wide. Water lilies that spread more than 10 feet wide are best for large ponds.

YOU SHOULD KNOW
Water lilies prefer still water. They don't grow well in moving water, such as in streams, nor do they grow well near waterfalls where water will splash their leaves. If you do have a waterfall, situate your water lily opposite the falls and away from the skimmer, if present, to ensure calm water and many blooms.

hardy varieties:

① **'TEXAS DAWN'** is a hardy water lily that blooms in shades of yellow. It grows 3 to 5 feet wide and is hardy in Zones 4–11.

② **'MARLIACEA CARNEA'** is a hardy water lily with blush pink flowers. Unlike many hardy water lilies, it will bloom in part shade. It grows 4 to 5 feet wide and is hardy in Zones 4–11.

All about hardy water lilies

Hardy water lilies are day bloomers. They open around 9 a.m. and close around 4 p.m. On dark, cloudy days, they may not open at all. Generally, their flowers rest on the water surface. Hardy water lily cultivars flower in a wide range of colors, from the darkest reds to the purest whites and in bright pinks and creamy yellow shades. The only colors missing are blues and purples. (If you would like to add these hues to your garden, grow tropical water lilies.)

Hardy water lilies flower when the pond temperature reaches 65°F. In cold climates where several weeks of warm weather are required for the water to reach 65°F, you can trick water lilies into blooming by moving them closer to the water surface. In extreme climates, position the water lilies about 3 inches below the surface to encourage them to begin blooming earlier in the season.

Planting hardy water lilies

Hardy water lilies have a thick fleshy root called a rhizome. To plant a bare-root hardy water lily, fill the planting container about three-fourths full of heavy garden soil and form a mound of soil in the center. Position the rhizome on the mound of soil at a 45-degree angle and spread the roots over the mound. Be sure the crown, where the stems and leaves will emerge, is pointing up.

Cover the roots and rhizome with a thin layer of soil, and tamp it down. Don't cover the crown. Water the soil thoroughly and top it with a ½-inch layer of pea gravel.

hardy varieties:

① **'JAMES BRYDON'** has deep red flowers that open in full sun or part shade. Its applelike fragrance is unique and appealing. It spreads 3 to 4 feet and grows well in small to large ponds. Hardy in Zones 4–11.

② **'GLADSTONIANA'** has pristine white petals. Its relatively few petals set it apart from larger, more complex blossoms. It spreads 5 to 8 feet and is best for medium to large ponds. Hardy in Zones 4–11.

③ **'COLORADO'** has fragrant, peach-color flowers that rise 3 to 4 inches above the water surface. This late bloomer begins flowering in August and continues into September. It spreads 3 to 5 feet. Hardy in Zones 4–11.

④ **'HELVOLA'** is a miniature water lily that produces pretty yellow flowers among leaves that are streaked with purple. It spreads 3 to 4 feet. Hardy in Zones 4–11.

Dividing water lilies

Water lilies are easy to divide. Divide plants in spring or early summer so the new plants have ample time to recover and harden off for winter. Begin by washing soil off the rhizome to find the small "eyes" that have sprouted here and there.

Look for eyes that have a few leaves and roots. Cut the entire eye, along with the roots and leaves, from the main root with a sharp knife. Let leafless eyes continue growing for later divisions. Plant the new sprouts in fresh soil so that the leaf sprouts are just at the soil level.

Overwintering hardy water lilies

Hardy water lilies are easy to overwinter in a pond that is 3 feet or deeper—simply move them to the deep zone for winter. It requires a bit more effort to overwinter them in shallow ponds. Here are a couple of different methods; choose the one that is easier for you.

The first method involves storing a water lily in its container in a protected location. After the first frost, remove the container with the water lily from the pond. Trim off all dead leaves and stems. Place the container in a plastic bag to maintain moisture. Store the water lily in a cool basement or other area where the temperature is between 32 and 50°F. Check the water lily periodically to make sure that there is plenty of moisture in the bag.

Hardy water lilies can also be overwintered in sphagnum moss (available at your local garden center). After the first frost remove the plant from the pond. Lift the rhizomes from the pot; prune off all old leaves and stems. Store the rhizomes in damp sphagnum moss placed in a plastic bag. Store the bag in a basement or other area where the temperature is 40 to 50°F.

hardy varieties:

① **'PEACH GLOW'** features large, luminous, peach-color flowers that turn pale yellow at the end of their four-day bloom period. This vigorous variety produces blooms into fall. It spreads 5 to 7 feet and is hardy in Zones 4–11.

② **'REMBRANDT'** has striking rose-pink blooms that age to dark red when the flowers are three to four days old. A good choice for medium to large ponds, it spreads 4 to 5 feet wide. Hardy in Zones 4–11.

③ **'LILY PONS'** boasts flowers with more than 100 petals and a pleasing, sweet fragrance. The 5- to 6-inch-wide pink flowers bloom above pads that extend to form a colony 4 to 5 feet wide. Hardy in Zones 4–11.

All about tropical water lilies

Your nose is likely to alert you to tropical water lilies before your eyes catch a glimpse of these exotic flowers. Sweetly fragrant tropical water lilies exude an almost intoxicating fragrance. In fact, they are often used in creating perfume.

Tropical water lilies flower much more than hardy water lilies. The most common color is blue, but they also come in a range of lavenders and purples, as well as pinks, yellows, and whites. Some are small and suitable for container water gardens. Other plants can grow more than 8 feet in diameter in a single season. Some tropical water lilies are known for their huge leaves—some measure more than 2 feet wide. The foliage is often mottled in purple or brown.

Tropical water lilies flower in the day or night, depending on the cultivar. If you primarily enjoy your water garden after work, consider planting night-blooming water lilies, which unfurl their petals late in the day and remain open for several hours after dusk.

Tropical water lilies flower when the water temperature reaches 70°F. Unlike hardy water lilies, which bloom for a couple weeks and then take a multiweek rest before blooming again, tropical water lilies bloom repeatedly as soon as the water temperature warms in summer. Trick the plants into blooming by elevating them to within about 6 inches of the water surface. The additional sunlight will spur early blooming.

Planting tropical water lilies

A little detective work is required to plant tropical water lilies at the right depth. Examine the plant's stems, starting at the base. Look for the point where the stem changes color from light to dark. This is the point at which the leaf emerged from the soil. When you plant the water lily, the pea gravel must be even with this point. This will ensure that you have the plant's growing crown (the union where the roots meet the stems) at the right depth.

tropical varieties:

1. **'TANZANITE'** is an award-winning water lily with deep violet flowers and showy mottled pads. It spreads 4 to 6 feet and is hardy in Zones 9–11.
2. **'BLUE BEAUTY'** is a day-blooming tropical with loads of sweetly fragrant flowers. This large, vigorous plant grows 5 to 7 feet wide and is best suited for medium to large ponds. Hardy in Zones 9–11.
3. **'MRS. GEORGE H. PRING'** features striking white flowers with a bright yellow center. The day-blooming flowers contrast beautifully with the mottled purple-and-green lily pads. It spreads 4 to 6 feet and is hardy in Zones 8–11.

After you find the plant's crown, the planting process is the same as for hardy water lilies. Fill the pot about three-fourths full of heavy garden soil, form a mound in the middle of the pot, place the base of the plant over the mound, and then spread out the roots and cover them with more soil. Leave enough room to top off the pot with a layer of pea gravel at the point of color change on the stem.

Making more tropical water lilies

In early summer, some water lilies produce young plants in the center of their leaves. This is called viviparous growth. Some day-blooming tropical water lilies are especially prone to doing this, as are a few hardy water lilies from time to time. Use a rock to pin the leaves that have sprouted plantlets to the soil surface. Once the plantlets sprout roots, cut off the old leaf and plant the new water lilies in their own pots.

Overwintering tropical water lilies

Tropical water lilies are easy to overwinter in an aquarium indoors. Before the first frost, remove the plants from the pond. Take the plants out of their containers and trim off all of the leaves and most of the roots. Repot the plants into smaller containers and store them in an aquarium tank or other container where they will receive plenty of light and the water temperature is consistently 68°F. In early summer, transplant the water lilies to larger containers and return them to the pond when the water temperature reaches 70°F.

tropical varieties:

1. **'PANAMA PACIFIC'** is a day-blooming tropical water lily that produces hundreds of lovely violet purple flowers over the course of a season. It has a sweet scent and plants spread 4 to 6 feet. Hardy in Zones 9–11.
2. **'AFTERGLOW'** is a tropical water lily that blooms in shades of pink, orange, and yellow. It grows 4 to 6 feet wide and is hardy in Zones 9–11.
3. **'HOT PINK'** has neon pink flowers that light up the garden during the day. This tropical water lily spreads 4 feet wide and is hardy in Zones 9–11.
4. **'SHIRLEY BYRNE'** is a day-blooming tropical cultivar with vibrant pink blooms. It spreads 4 to 6 feet, and its flowers rise several inches above the water surface. Hardy in Zones 9–11.
5. **'RED FLARE'** is a spectacular night-blooming water lily with 7- to 10-inch-wide red flowers. Plants spread 5 to 6 feet. Hardy in Zones 9–11.

Water mint
(*Mentha aquatica*)

Very fragrant and easy to grow, water mint forms a low-growing carpet of green foliage at the edge of ponds and streams. The foliage can be used in teas and jellies.

Where to plant

Water mint grows well in full sun or part shade. It succeeds in moist soil or submerged a couple inches below the water surface. The plant grows 3 to 12 inches tall and spreads by vigorous running stems. It is hardy in Zones 5 to 11.

Growing

Because water mint, like all mints, is a rampant grower, plant it in a container where its spread will be somewhat confined. Clusters of small blue or pink flowers decorate the plant in summer and fall.

Special notes

Brook mint (*M. pulegium*) is a ½-inch-tall version of water mint. It has airy, sky blue flowers. Brook mint is as fragrant as other mints and when in bloom it attracts butterflies.

Water pennywort
(*Hydrocotyle* spp.)

Low-growing water pennywort creates a soft carpet of foliage between the edge of the pond and tall pond plants. You'll love its unique round leaves.

Where to plant

Plant water pennywort in full sun or part shade. It grows 1 to 4 inches tall and spreads quickly by running stems that float over the water surface. Water pennywort grows in moist soil or submerged up to 4 inches below the water surface. It is hardy in Zones 7 to 11.

Growing

Plant water pennywort in a shallow container filled with heavy garden soil. For tender species grown in cold climates, take 6-inch-long stem cuttings in fall. Place the cuttings in a glass filled with water. When placed in a sunny window, the cuttings will root quickly. Overwinter them indoors and plant in the pond after all chance of freeze has passed. Cold-tolerant species overwinter well at the bottom of the pond.

Special notes

Hairy pennywort (*H. americana*) is one of the few pennyworts with noticeable flowers, that rise above the foliage in white tufts. It trails freely and is an excellent plant for waterfalls, pond edges, tub gardens, or tabletop gardens.

YOU SHOULD KNOW
Trailing plants like water pennywort and parrot's feather are excellent choices for container gardens. They will quickly scramble over the edge of the pot, giving the container garden a lush appearance.

Water willow
(*Justicia americana*)

A great backdrop for bold water lilies and lotuses, water willow has a pleasing shrublike habit and thrives in shallow water. It has clusters of pink to white flowers in summer.

Where to plant

Water willow grows best in moist soil or submerged in several inches of water. It tolerates running water. The plant stands about 18 inches tall and spreads about 12 inches wide. It is hardy in Zones 4 to 11.

Growing

Plant water willow in a container filled with heavy garden soil in early spring. After the plant establishes a strong root system, trim it as needed to maintain the necessary size and shape. Divide rhizomes in early spring before new growth appears.

Special notes

Water willow is occasionally used along shorelines to prevent erosion. When using it in the water garden, plant it in a container to prevent overexuberant spread.

White-top sedge
(*Rhynchospora colorata*)

The star-shape white seedheads of white-top sedge float above grasslike foliage. Its spiky shape adds great texture to plant combinations. It grows in water or moist soil.

Where to plant

Plant white-top sedge in full sun or part shade. It grows 1 to 2 feet tall and spreads vigorously by runners. The plant grows well in moist soil or submerged up to 1 inch below the water surface. It is hardy in Zones 8 to 11.

Growing

White-top sedge has a vigorous running habit and is best confined to a container. Plant it in a shallow pot filled with heavy garden soil. Divide plants every few years to maintain vigor. After blooming in summer, the flowers and the surrounding spikes turn light brown, retaining their starlike appearance.

White-top sedge overwinters easily and requires no special treatment. In cold climates overwinter plants indoors.

Special notes

R. colorata is closely related to *R. latifolia*, and the two are often sold interchangeably at nurseries and garden centers. The white seedheads of *R. latifolia* are about one-third larger than those of *R. colorata*.

USDA Plant Hardiness Zone Map

Each plant has an ability to withstand cold temperatures.

This range of temperatures is expressed as a zone—and a zone map shows where you can grow this plant.

Planting for your zone

There are 11 zones from Canada to Mexico, and each zone represents the lowest expected winter temperature in that area. Each zone is based on a 10-degree difference in minimum temperatures. Once you know your hardiness zone, you can choose plants for your garden that will flourish. Look for the hardiness zone on the plant tags of the water garden plants you buy.

Microclimates in your yard

Not all areas in your yard are the same. Depending on your geography, trees, and structures, some spots may receive different sunlight and wind and consequently experience temperature differences. Take a look around your yard and you may notice that the same plant comes up sooner in one place than another. This is the microclimate concept in action. A microclimate is an area in your yard that is slightly different (cooler or hotter) than the other areas of your yard.

Create a microclimate

Once you're aware of your yard's microclimates, use them to your advantage. For example, you may be able to grow plants in a sheltered, south-facing garden bed that you can't grow elsewhere in your yard. You can create a microclimate by planting evergreens on the north side of your property to block prevailing winds. Or plant deciduous trees on the south side to provide shade in summer.

Above: **Check the zone rating on water lilies and other plants to determine if they need special care to overwinter in your garden.**

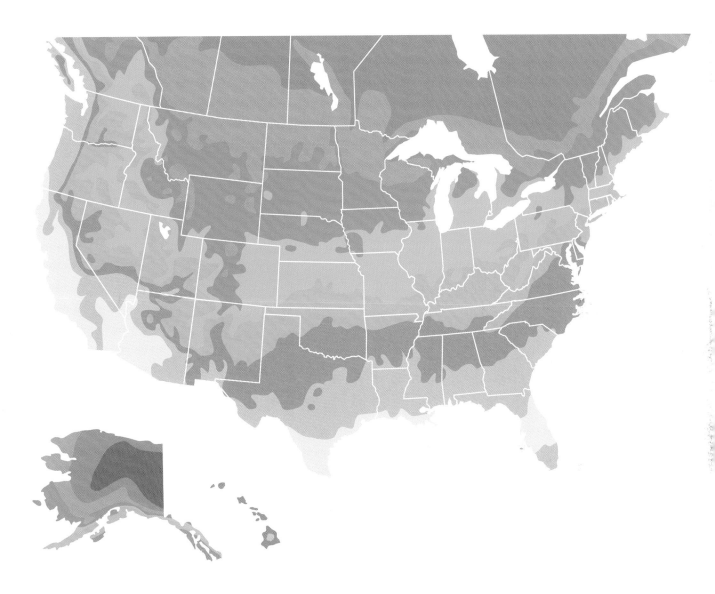

Range of Average Annual Minimum Temperatures for Each Zone

- ■ Zone 1: below -50°F (below -45.6°C)
- ■ Zone 2: -50 to -40°F (-45 to -40°C)
- ■ Zone 3: -40 to -30°F (-40 to -35°C)
- ■ Zone 4: -30 to -20°F (-34 to -29°C)
- ■ Zone 5: -20 to -10°F (-29 to -23°C)
- ■ Zone 6: -10 to 0°F (-23 to -18°C)
- ■ Zone 7: 0 to 10°F (-18 to -12°C)
- ■ Zone 8: 10 to 20°F (-12 to -7°C)
- ■ Zone 9: 20 to 30°F (-7 to -1°C)
- ■ Zone 10: 30 to 40°F (-1 to 4°C)
- ■ Zone 11: 40°F and above (4.5°C and above)

Resources

Mail order water garden supplies
Look for aquatic plants and water gardening supplies at local garden centers and retail outlets, but when you can't find a particular product, turn to water gardening and plant specialists. Search online for specialists or use one of these reputable retailers. Some sell nationally; some do not. Visit websites or call for more information.

AQUASCAPE
www.aquascapeinc.com
Specializes in pond products and installation

CALIFORNIA CARNIVORES
2833 Old Gravenstein Highway South
Sebastopol, CA 95472
(707) 824-0433
www.californiacarnivores.com
Specializes in carnivorous plants

KLOUBEC KOI FARM
1375 Baxter Avenue NW
Amana, IA 52203
(888) 564-4692
www.klousbeckoi.com
Specializes in koi and koi care products

LILYBLOOMS AQUATIC GARDENS
932 South Main Street
North Canton, OH 44720
(800) 921-0005
www.lilyblooms.com
Specializes in pond equipment and aquatic plants

LILYPONS WATER GARDENS
6800 Lily Pons Road
Adamstown, MD 21710
(800) 999-5459
www.lilypons.com
Specializes in aquatic plants

LECHUZA
(877) 532-4892
www. lechuza.com
Specializes in containers for water gardens

LIQUID LANDSCAPE DESIGNERS
9401 Northwest 70th Avenue
Johnston, IA 50131
(877) 796-7663
www.liquidlandscapedesigners.com
Specializes in water garden installation

NATURAL ENVIRONMENTAL SYSTEMS, LLC
5000 Quorum Drive #300
Dallas, TX 75254
(800) 999-9345
www.naturalenviro.com
Specializes in earth-friendly water additives

PARADISE WATER GARDENS
14 May Street
Whitman, MA 02382
(800) 955-0161
www.paradisewatergardens.com
Specializes in pond liners and aquatic plants

PERRY'S WATER GARDEN
136 Gibson Aquatic Farm Road
Franklin, NC 28734
(828) 524-3264
www.perryswatergarden.net
Specializes in aquatic plants

PLANT DELIGHTS NURSERY, INC.
9241 Sauls Road
Raleigh, NC 27603
(919) 772-4794
www.plantdelights.com
Specializes in unique perennials

POND WORLD
1018 W Cherry Avenue
Enid, OK 73703
(866) 897-2307
www.pondworld.com
Specializes in pond equipment

SMARTPOND
(888) 755-4497
www.smart-pond.com
Specializes in pond supplies; distributed by Lowe's stores

TEXAS WATER LILIES
25999 North Lake Road
Waller, TX 77484
(936) 931-9880
www.texaswaterlilies.com
Specializes in water lilies

UTOPIA AQUATIC, LLC
P.O. Box 2242
Riverview, FL 33568
(800) 390-1590
utopiaaquatic.com
Specializes in tropical water lilies

WHITE FLOWER FARM
P.O. Box 50, Route 63
Litchfield, CT 06759
(800) 503-9624
www.whiteflowerfarm.com
Specializes in perennial plants

WILLIAM TRICKER, INC.
7125 Tanglewood Drive
Independence, OH 44131
(800) 524-3492
www.tricker.com
Specializes in water garden equipment, fish, and
   aquatic plants

Water gardening groups
Connect with other water gardeners. National
and international societies might have local
groups in your area where you can learn about
water gardening techniques specific to your
growing region.

**INTERNATIONAL WATERLILY AND WATER
GARDENING SOCIETY**
7443 Buffalo Road
Churchville, NY 14428
(585) 293-9144
www.iwgs.org

Gardening tools and supplies
Look for gardening tools and supplies at local
nurseries and garden centers. The following
mail order suppliers also carry a range of garden
specialty supplies.

A.M. LEONARD
241 Fox Drive
Piqua, OH 45356
(800) 543-8955
www.amleo.com

GARDENER'S SUPPLY COMPANY
128 Intervale Road
Burlington, VT 05401
(888) 833-1412
www.gardeners.com

GARDENS ALIVE!
5100 Schenley Place
Lawrenceburg, IN 47025
(513) 354-1482
www.gardensalive.com

LEE VALLEY TOOLS LTD.
P.O. Box 1780
Ogdensburg, NY 13669
(800) 267-8735
www.leevalley.com

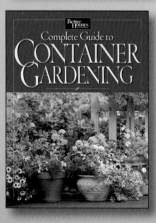

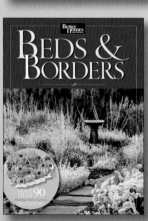

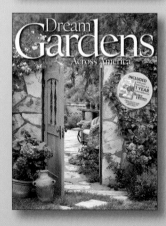

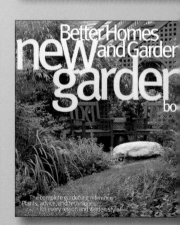
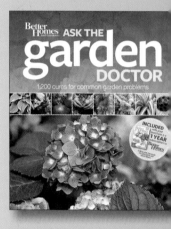